Please Don't Hurt Me

Dr. Grant Martin

NOTE

Most of the illustrations used in this book are drawn from true case histories. Names, gender, and other identifying information have been changed to protect the actual people involved.

Unless otherwise indicated, Scripture quotations are from the *Holy Bible, New International Version,* © 1973, 1978, 1984, International Bible Society. Used by permission of Zondervan Bible Publishers. Other quotations are from the *King James Version* (KJV).

Recommended Dewey Decimal Classification: 364.15
Suggested Subject Heading: ABUSE

Library of Congress Catalog Card Number: 86-63144
ISBN: 0-89693-743-7

Cover photo by Carlos Vergara.

VICTOR BOOKS
A division of SP Publications, Inc.
Wheaton, Illinois 60187

CONTENTS

DEDICATION

To my parents, "L.B." and Thelma,
who gave me a violence-free home,
tender loving care,
and the freedom to make choices.

PREFACE

A scream of fright. Muffled cries. Bruises and broken bones. Emotional scars that last a lifetime. These are responses to violence.

When we hear the word *violence,* most of us think of murder, terrorist attacks, rape, armed robbery, and muggings—events we read about every day in our newspapers. But there is a far more frequent and equally devastating kind of violence. It is family violence and includes spouse abuse, abuse of children, and mistreatment of the elderly.

This book is intended to help those who have been victims of family violence or who are concerned for those who may have been victimized. It is not a textbook laden with theory and hypotheses about the causes of violence within the family, but a practical and sensitive presentation of how to cope.

Please Don't Hurt Me is divided into two parts. The first section deals with child abuse, particularly child sexual abuse. It is for parents (or caretakers) who want to prevent their child from being abused as well as for those whose child has been abused. The discussion focuses on how to identify an abused child and what to do if abuse is suspected.

Part 2 of the book discusses abused spouses, particularly battered wives; adults who have been sexually abused as children; and abuse of the elderly. Included are practical and caring ideas for dealing both with the crisis situation and the long-term resolution of the trauma.

This book was not an enjoyable one to write. I did not set out to specialize in family violence. But in the past several years, my work with children and families has forced me to deal with abuse in all its forms. Consequently, I made a decision, somewhat clothed in righteous indignation, to do all I could to stem the tide of this silent stalker of the helpless and dependent. Preparing this book for victims of abuse has been part of my battle plan.

Tears are meant to be signs of sorrow, grief, temporary pain, and joy, not a constant companion of those who face chronic mistreatment. My prayer is that those who hurt will, by the grace of God, experience the healing touch of the Master's hand and be transformed from victims to victors.

GRANT L. MARTIN
Seattle, Washington
1987

PART 1

A Child Is Crying

CHAPTER ONE

Why Are the Children Crying?

The Nature and Scope of Child Abuse

Babies cry because something is wrong. They are telling their caretakers they are hungry, wet, sleepy, or have a pain. In fact, it's the only way infants can communicate their needs to the world. Loving parents will respond to their child's cry with comforting action and concern. An abused child's tears will often be met with more violence or neglect.

Screams of fright can accompany broken bones, scalding water, or glowing cigarettes placed against the child's flesh. Tears of terror may represent spleens ruptured by repeated blows or skin welted and bruised by merciless whippings. A child may cry because of inflamed sexual organs or because his trust bond with a parent has been broken.

Most babies get their bottles or eventually have their diapers changed. But thousands of infants and children experience trauma and abuse that will scar them for a lifetime.

> Jan once spent a year in a military stockade for beating her young son and now has pleaded guilty to a charge of first-degree assault involving a second attack on the child—this

time with a broom handle. The second charge stems from an assault in which her five-year-old son was so severely beaten that he suffered brain damage. When the child was brought to a hospital for treatment, he was unconscious and covered with welts, bruises, rope burns, and bite marks.

And what of Jan's own past? Her stepfather began molesting her when she was nine. It started with Ken touching her genitals while the two of them were alone, watching TV. The abuse progressed to fondling when Ken would tuck Jan into bed at night. Jan missed her natural father, who left town after divorcing her mother five years previously. She liked Ken, and found the touching strange, yet soothing.

Jan's mother, Helen, and Ken were always fighting. Helen realized she had made a mistake in marrying Ken, but had vowed to give Jan a decent home. Ken was a good provider and Helen couldn't stand the prospect of being on her own again. As a result, Ken and Helen seldom spent quality time together. By the time Jan was eleven, Helen devoted as much time as possible to church and community activities just so she wouldn't have to be around Ken.

Ken's sexual activity with Jan progressed in scope and intensity throughout her fifth and sixth grades. When she entered junior high, Ken tried to restrict Jan's friends. Jan resented her stepfather's restraints and became increasingly more defiant and angry. She resisted his advances more strongly, but never told her mother about the abuse. Jan didn't think her mother would believe her anyway. Many nights, Jan would cry herself to sleep because of her confusion and sense of hopelessness.

Abuse fosters abuse. The cries of one generation of family violence become the cries of the next.

HOW MANY CHILDREN ARE CRYING?

The National Center on Child Abuse and Neglect estimates over 1 million children are abused or neglected *each year.* One hundred thousand to 200,000 are physically abused, 100,000 to 200,000 are sexually abused, and the remainder are physically or educationally neglected.[1] About 2,000 children are killed each year because of abuse or neglect by their parents or caretakers.

Abused children can be found at all socioeconomic levels and the overall incidence rates are similar for city, suburban, and rural communities.[2]

I could report many more statistics to illustrate the magnitude of the problem. The bottom line is that children are crying by the millions. Not just because they need a diaper changed or a bottle of milk, but because they have been hit, burned, sexually molested, and neglected.

WHAT MAKES THE CHILDREN CRY?

Because of the national level of concern, in 1974 the United States Congress passed the Child Abuse Prevention and Treatment Act. The purpose of this act was to create a nationwide system to encourage research into ways to prevent and treat child abuse and neglect. The law defined child abuse and neglect as:

> the physical or mental injury, sexual abuse or exploitation, negligent treatment, or maltreatment of a child under the age of eighteen, by a person who is responsible for the child's welfare and under circumstances which indicate the child's health or welfare is harmed or threatened thereby.

What makes child abuse and neglect different from other crimes is that the abuser is a parent, custodian, or guardian. Child abuse is not the act of weird-looking strangers, but of someone empowered with the duty to protect and guide the child to normal adulthood. A violation of trust takes place in many crimes, but the implications are more profound when the bond is broken by a parent or entrusted caretaker.

Four types of abuse are pinpointed in the federal law. Each of these is illustrated hereafter, followed by definitions taken from the law.

1. *Physical abuse.* Elise was a difficult child from the day she was born. Her mother, Heidi, had really wanted a boy, and Elise had colic and food allergies almost constantly. Heidi's husband worked nights and needed quiet to sleep during the day, which

11

compounded the problem. Both parents believed it was important to be firm with children so they would not become headstrong and defiant.

When Elise was about two years old, her mother began trying to toilet train her. Heidi would ask her daughter if she had to go to the bathroom, and Elise would repeatedly say no. Almost invariably, Elise would wet or soil her diapers. Heidi was furious. One day, after a number of other irritations, Heidi checked Elise's pants and found a mess. Out of frustration, Heidi forced Elise to sit on top of a hot heater grate to teach her a lesson. It left a series of wafflelike burns on her bottom.

Physical abuse is violent assault with an implement such as a knife or strap, as well as burns, fractures, and other intent-to-harm actions. Spanking for purely disciplinary reasons is usually not seen as child abuse.

2. *Neglect.* The caseworker knocked at the front door of the well-kept, two-story house in the suburbs. No one answered. Her call had been prompted by the local school principal who was concerned that Sally, the second-grader living here, had not been to school for two weeks. The school had received no explanation and could make no contact with the parents.

Finding the door unlocked, the caseworker poked her head inside the hallway and heard the sound of a TV. She walked to the next room and found Sally huddled under a blanket, still in her pajamas.

A further investigation found both parents were leaving for work before Sally got up each morning. She was on her own to get ready for school and walk the two blocks to the school bus stop. Several weeks ago, Sally had been teased by some older kids at the bus stop, so she decided not to go to school anymore. Her parents, busy with their own concerns, never knew their daughter had a problem.

Child neglect may be further classified as physical or educational. *Physical neglect* includes abandonment; refusal to seek, allow, or provide treatment for illness or impairment; inadequate physical supervision; disregard of health hazards in the home; and inadequate nutrition, clothing, or hygiene when services are available. *Educational neglect* includes knowingly permitting chronic truancy, keeping the child home from school repeatedly without cause, or failing to enroll a child in school.

3. Emotional abuse. Phillip's mother had been hospitalized for severe depression numerous times over the years. When the school social worker came to the home because of Phillip's hostile behavior and lack of classroom progress, the mother was still in bed. As the interview progressed, the social worker became increasingly aware that Mrs. Putman did not know much about Phillip's daily schedule or activities. Mr. Putman was on the road most of the time, and all of the child-rearing responsibilities were on the mother's shoulders. However, Phillip's mother was barely able to keep herself functioning, let alone keep up with a twelve-year-old boy.

Emotional abuse includes verbal or emotional assault; close confinement such as tying or locking in a closet; inadequate nurturance such as that affecting failure-to-thrive babies; knowingly permitting antisocial behavior such as delinquency, or serious alcohol/drug abuse; or refusal to allow medical care for a diagnosed emotional problem.

4. Sexual abuse. Jan's story of incest by a stepfather, mentioned at the beginning of this chapter, illustrates one type of child sexual abuse. Sexual abuse also includes molestation, and exploitation for prostitution or the production of pornographic materials.

Legally, child sexual abuse can be described in several ways. It can be called *rape* if physical force is used and penetration takes place, or *statutory rape* if force is not used and the victim is under age. Sexual abuse without penetration, such as touching, fondling, and masturbation, usually is defined as *indecent liberties.*

From a psychological perspective, child sexual abuse is the sexual exploitation of a child who is not developmentally capable of understanding or resisting the contact, and/or who is psychologically and socially dependent on the offender.

Two criteria establish child sexual abuse as a form of violence. The first is the lack of consent on the part of the victim. For children, the lack of consent is a given. They cannot give or withhold consent when approached sexually by an adult, because they are immature, uninformed, and usually dependent on the adult. They lack any real power to resist or make choices.

A ten-year-old child who is exploited by her father,[3] for example, has no options. If the adult who is supposed to be her prime protector is also her exploiter, where can she go? This is the power an adult, particularly a parent, has over a child. Adults have an element of choice in regards to sexual conduct, but children do not.

The second criterion for seeing sexual abuse as a form of violence is the resultant injury to the victim. The sexual use of a child disregards the child's best welfare. The child becomes an object exclusively to meet the needs of the offender. The act is exploitative and, therefore, damaging to the child.

A common fallout of sexual abuse is the intense betrayal of trust. When the trust of a child is turned into corrupted obedience in order to meet the selfish desires of the adult, a legacy of suspicion and hurt is created. Many women, abused as children, undergo years of therapy learning to cope with a life in which they will never have an earthly, loving, caring father.

HOW LONG HAVE CHILDREN BEEN CRYING?

Since time immemorial, children have been treated with incredible cruelty. Children have been tortured, burned, worked to death, terrorized, and flogged daily in order to "discipline" them. Infants have been dipped in icewater and rolled in the snow in order to "harden" them, as well as buried alive with their dead parents.

Parents have been "beating the devil" out of their children since colonial times. Many communities enacted "stubborn child laws," which gave parents the right to kill children who were beyond their ability to control.[4]

Parents have exposed children to weather, and starved or abandoned them in order to avoid the burden of rearing them or having to divide property among too many heirs. The Huns used to cut the cheeks of newborn males; Italian Renaissance parents would burn a child's neck with a hot iron or drop burning candle wax on newborn babies. It was common to cut the string under the newborn's tongue, often with the midwife's fingernail. In every age, the deliberate mutilation of children's bones and faces prepared them for a lifetime of begging.

In Roman times, parents would leave unwanted babies at the foot of certain columns to die or to be taken by derelicts and raised as prostitutes or beggars. During the 17th and 18th centuries, large numbers of children were forced into workhouses where all but the strongest died.

Certain characteristics have historically contributed to the value of an individual child. Firstborn, healthy males have always held a higher value. Girls were more likely to be left exposed or to be killed than boys. Indeed, it was rare for more than one girl in a family to be spared. Children found to be mentally retarded, physically handicapped, born as a twin, conceived out of wedlock, or perhaps just born into a poor family have been in most jeopardy throughout history.[5]

A child's life prior to modern times was very bleak. Most every child-rearing manual from antiquity to the 18th century recommended the beating of children. It was common at home and school. One 19th-century German schoolmaster even kept score of his actions. He administered 911,527 strokes with a stick, 124,000 lashes with a whip, 136,715 slaps with his hand, and 1,115,800 boxes on the ear.[6]

Fairy tales, folklore, and nursery rhymes are full of violence against children. Hansel and Gretel's parents left them to starve in the forest when money got scarce. At the orders of the wicked queen, Snow White was taken to the forest by huntsmen, where they were told to cut out her heart.

The incidence of physical abuse to children is also found in both the Old and New Testaments. Pharaoh, king of Egypt, advised the Hebrew midwives to kill every Hebrew boy (Exodus 1:16), and when that scheme didn't work, he then demanded all boys be thrown into the river (v. 22).

Judges 9:5 records that Abimelech murdered seventy of his brothers. Second Chronicles 28:3 indicates that Ahaz sacrificed his sons in the fire. Another passage makes reference to the pagan practices of abandoning infants and exposing them to the elements: "You were thrown out into the open field, for on the day you were born you were despised" (Ezekiel 16:5).

In the New Testament accounts, King Herod, hoping to eliminate the Messiah, ordered all boys under age two, in and around Bethlehem to be killed (Matthew 2:16).

The treatment of children today is more humane than at any other time in history. However, it's possible the functional equivalents of earlier modes of neglect are still with us. We don't send infants out to wet nurses at birth, or to be servants at age seven. But we do abandon them to hosts of nurseries, preschools, teachers, camps, and baby-sitters for a major part of their young

15

lives. We don't throw dead babies into latrines or rivers, but we abort the lives of fetuses by the thousands, sometimes using back-alley garbage bins for disposal.[7]

FREQUENCY AND HISTORY OF CHILD SEXUAL ABUSE

Child sexual abuse will be the major focus of the remaining chapters of Part 1. While any type of abuse leaves its scars, sexual abuse has only in the past few years become known to have victimized literally millions of children. The sexual abuse of children is one of the most underreported forms of child maltreatment. And since it often goes undetected, its impact may not become evident for years. There is often no physical evidence of harm. Also, children do not report sexual abuse because of ignorance, fear of reprisal or blame, or guilt over any pleasure they may have experienced. To a great degree, child sexual abuse remains a conspiracy of silence. The purpose of this book is to offer comfort and assistance to those thousands of children and adults who have been shedding silent tears as a result of their abuse.

It has been estimated that one in every six people has been involved in some form of incestuous relationship. One study found sexual abuse has occurred among 38 percent of a large group of women before they were eighteen and among 28 percent before they were fourteen.[8] This amounts to as many as 250,000 children molested each year!

Eighty percent of the victims of child sexual abuse are female, though it is expected that abuse of male children is underreported. The embarrassment and shame that tends to deter girls from reporting such abuse has an even greater effect on boys, since the abuse is often homosexual.

The initial sexual abuse may occur at any age, from infancy through adolescence. However, the largest number of reported cases involves females under age eleven. The sexual activity is usually repetitive and progressive. There is no escape for the victim until he or she is old enough to realize that incest is not a common or appropriate experience for a child, and until he or she is strong enough to obtain help outside the family.

Unfortunately, the evidence suggests that the frequency of child sexual abuse is as high within the church community as it is in the secular community.

It's difficult to measure someone's level of Christianity, but many counselors, therapists, and researchers do report that the adult male offenders tend to be very devout, moralistic, and conservative in their religious beliefs.

In my study on family violence, I have talked to sexual assault center employees, college counselors, therapists, and researchers up and down the West Coast and across the Midwest. They are unanimous that the rate of sexual abuse is no less in religious or Christian homes than among the general public. One counselor from a Christian university told me a major portion of his student caseload was for problems related to sexual abuse. He felt that one out of ten was a conservative estimate for abused female students on his campus.

One author, herself a victim of incest by a father who was an active member of a fundamentalist church, reports a survey of female students at a Christian liberal arts college. Of the students who responded to the survey, more than half said they had been abused as children. Almost all of those students had been reared in Christian homes.[9]

A study completed at Pasadena's Fuller Graduate School of Psychology surveyed 900 Christian counselors and pastors on the subject of family sexual abuse. The majority of those who responded to the questionnaire felt that incest occurred as often in Christian as in non-Christian homes.[10]

While we might not like to admit it, this form of family violence may be even more prevalent within the church community than any other kind of abuse. Somehow, the addictive nature of sexual abuse has found a relatively safe breeding ground within many parts of the church.

HISTORY OF CHILD SEXUAL ABUSE

Secular history is replete with child sexual abuse. Greek poetry abounds with tales of men swooning for "the tender flower of youth." Young boys were valued for their softness and sometimes castrated in hopes they would remain tender and delicate.

The Roman emperor, Tiberius, enjoyed molesting and swimming with young boys. Many children during the Middle Ages were loaned out for sexual services.

The technological inventiveness of the 19th century, along with the Victorian male's interest in young girls spurred the production and distribution of child pornography. As late as 1832, children were considered victims of rape only if they were under ten years of age.

Perverse men have always found ways to take advantage of the status and availability of children. During the middle 1800s, as many as 2,000 young immigrant girls would disappear each year in New York City, victims of sex merchants.

Incest was strictly prohibited in the Old Testament law (Leviticus 18:6-18). Rape was likewise forbidden, and death established as a consequence (Deuteronomy 22:25-27). But Scripture records that the Israelites often stumbled.

Genesis records Dinah's rape by Shechem (34:2) and Reuben sleeping with Bilhah, his father's concubine (35:22). Incest was the sin when Amnon raped his sister Tamar (2 Samuel 13:14). What followed is an early example of the minimizing of the trauma of sexual abuse, so common in current times, for after Tamar reported her attack and subsequent shame to Absalom, her brother, he advised her to remain quiet and keep the family secret (v. 20). And though King David was incensed by his daughter's rape, there is no record that he ever took any action against Amnon. Perhaps the memory of David's own sin with Bathsheba kept him from punishing his son.

Later, we read about Absalom's own violation of the law when he committed incest with his father's concubines (2 Samuel 16:22).

Another instance of rape involved the Levite's concubine (Judges 19:25-28). Abused by a gang of angry young men, she died from the shock of the ordeal.

Many prostitutes have been abused as children. It is estimated that over 75 percent of all adolescents involved in prostitution, both male and female, were victims of prior sexual violence, rape, incestuous abuse, or molestation.[11] It is assumed that these traumas led to their decision to work the streets.

Though Ezekiel 23 is probably an allegory of the unfaithfulness of Israel, the illustration of two adulterous sisters, Oholah and Oholibah, nevertheless is a sad one. While still young children, they became prostitutes in Egypt, and suffered all manner of indignities. Even as a parable, the inference can be made that sexual abuse of young girls was common in Old Testament cultures.

The Apostle Paul referred to the problem of incest in the church at Corinth and admonished the leadership for not taking action to remove the offending parties from the fellowship (1 Corinthians 5:1-2).

* * * * *

Millions of children are crying in silence. Their tears represent physical, sexual, and emotional abuse and neglect that has been occurring for centuries. Not only must we do everything possible to stop their abuse, we need to minister to their hurts and scars. The following chapters will detail some of the hows and whys of child sexual abuse. Knowledge about the conditions and perpetrators of abuse will help you identify high-risk situations and enable you to take preventative action. Specific suggestions will also be given for what to do if you discover your, or someone else's, child has been abused. In Part 2, chapters 7 and 8 deal with the long-term effects of adults abused as children.

The tragedy of child abuse is a clear and certain fact. My prayer is that the church community will open its eyes to the pain of abused children and take action to prevent more unnecessary tears, as well as provide needed comfort and healing to those already victimized.

NOTES

1. National Center on Child Abuse and Neglect, *Executive Summary: National Study of the Incidence and Severity of Child Abuse and Neglect,* U.S. Department of Health and Human Services, December, 1980.
   American Association for Protecting Children, "Reports of Child Maltreatment Increase Again," 1985.
2. National Center on Child Abuse and Neglect, *Executive Summary,* 1980.
3. Because the majority of reported cases of child sexual abuse, particularly incest, involve females as victims, the feminine gender will be used in most references.

4. Murray A. Straus, Richard J. Gelles, and Suzanne K. Steinmetz, *Behind Closed Doors: Violence in the American Family* (Garden City, N.Y.: Anchor Books, 1980), pp. 51-52.
5. Pamela D. Mayhall and Katherine E. Norgard, *Child Abuse and Neglect: Sharing Responsibility* (New York: John Wiley, 1983), pp. 2-5.
6. Lloyd DeMause, "Our Forebears Made Childhood a Nightmare," in *Traumatic Abuse and Neglect of Children,* Gertrude Williams and John Money, eds. (Baltimore: Johns Hopkins, 1982), p. 14.
7. Mary Dunn, "500 Fetal Bodies Found," *The National Catholic Register,* February 21, 1982, p. 1.
8. Diana E. Russell, "The Incidence and Prevalence of Intrafamilial and Extrafamilial Abuse of Female Children," *Child Abuse and Neglect,* vol. 7, no. 2, 1983, pp. 133-146.
9. Randy Frame, "Child Abuse: The Church's Best Kept Secret?" *Christianity Today,* February 15, 1985, pp. 32-34.
10. Phyllis P. Hart and Mary Rotzien, "Survey of Pastors and Counselors on Incest." Paper read at Christian Association for Psychological Studies, Dallas, May, 1984.
11. Jennifer James, "Entrance into Juvenile Prostitution," University of Washington, August, 1980; and "Entrance into Juvenile Male Prostitution," University of Washington, August, 1982.

CHAPTER TWO

Hearing Their Cries

Identifying Victims of Child Sexual Abuse

Do we unknowingly teach our children the very qualities that make them prime victims of abuse? We want our children to be loving and kind. We tell them to respect authority, obey adults, and not to talk about their body parts. Parents have traditionally encouraged children to be seen and not heard. We have cautioned our children not to talk to strangers, but have encouraged them to be friendly to family members. Now we find almost all sexual abuse is committed by someone the child knows, often a father or stepfather. Have we done it all wrong?

What is the solution? Must we change our instruction and tell our children not to trust authority, never touch, and never stay alone with a parent? No simple formula guarantees freedom from harm, but part of the answer comes through knowledge. Scripture tells us, "My people are destroyed from lack of knowledge. Because you have rejected knowledge, I also reject you as My priests; because you have ignored the law of your God, I also will ignore your children" (Hosea 4:6).

As concerned parents and caretakers, we share a responsibility to instruct our children in ways that will help keep them safe.

Please Don't Hurt Me

God's Word tells us to be self-controlled and alert because the devil prowls around like a roaring lion looking for someone to devour (1 Peter 5:8).

This chapter describes the typical victims of child sexual abuse and some of the circumstances that seem highly related to instances of abuse. Knowledge of who risks being abused is the first step to prevention.

WHO ARE THE VICTIMS OF CHILD SEXUAL ABUSE?

Shannon was born after her mother had left Shannon's father. They had never married and her mom finally got the courage to escape the boyfriend's drinking and violent temper. After living alone for several years, Shannon's mother, Christie, married. The new stepfather had several children of his own, including a teenage son. Several years later, the mother became suspicious of certain activity between her seventeen-year-old stepson and Shannon. Upon confronting him, Christie obtained enough information to believe her daughter had been sexually abused. CPS caseworkers later obtained a full confession from the teenager, implicating him in severe molestation over the prior twelve months.

Through tears of sorrow and guilt, Christie told her child's counselor how, in looking back, she could identify many of the physical and emotional symptoms. Because of abuse in her own history, Christie had denied the possibility of danger in her current family. If only she had opened her eyes, perhaps she could have prevented this tragic episode.

Knowledge. If Christie had taken the time to study her situation she would have realized that many of the components of a high-risk situation were present.

Victims of child sexual abuse include both boys and girls, though girls predominate. Recent studies suggest the number of reported male sexual assaults is increasing. A Detroit study found 49 percent of the city's victims of child sexual assault in 1982 were boys and 51 percent were girls. While other studies have not shown the same equal distribution, the reporting of male victims is definitely on the rise.[1]

Estimates indicate perhaps 2.5 to 8.7 percent of all boys are sexually victimized. However, these same studies suggest two to three cases of female abuse are reported for every boy.[2]

Men are the abusers 95 percent of the time when the victim is female; men are the abusers 80 percent of the time when the victim is male.

The most common ages of those abused are between eight and twelve, though any age child can be victimized.[3]

A recent study of 365 adults molested as children found the ages at which abuse is most likely to occur were five, seven, and eight. Eighty-nine percent of the victims were female; 11 percent were male. That same study found that 39 percent of the offenders were the fathers of the victims and 23 percent were stepfathers. Ninety-nine percent of the offenders were known to the child, shattering the myth that sexual abuse is committed by strangers. Men were the perpetrators of the abuse 97 percent of the time in this study. Also, fondling from the waist down was the most common type of molestation.

Two additional findings of this study were that the abuse was reported in only 17.8 percent of the cases and the average number of years the victim waited before seeking help was seventeen.[4] This again illustrates the extent of the silent crime brought against children who are too afraid or powerless to defend themselves.

The almost 18 percent reporting rate from this study is high when compared to other surveys which found sexual abuse was only reported 2 to 6 percent of the time.[5]

Several researchers have substantiated the notion that stepfathers are inclined to be more sexually predatory toward their stepdaughters. One study found a stepfather was five times more likely to sexually victimize his stepdaughter than was a natural father. Another found that one out of six women who had a stepfather was sexually abused by him, compared to a rate of one out of forty abused by biological fathers.[6]

This same study also found girls with stepfathers were five times more likely to be victimized by a friend of her parents. The explanation given is that friends of the stepfather may not have felt the same kind of restraint they might have if this were the natural daughter of their friend. Also possible is that a mother who was dating actively may have put her daughter in jeopardy through the men she brought into the home.

A Canadian study found preschool children living with a step-parent were forty times more likely to become victims of abuse than children living with both natural parents. This would apparently include all types of abuse, not just sexual abuse. Another finding of the Canadian study was that preschool children living in single-parent homes are 12.5 times more likely to become abuse victims than children living with both natural parents.[7] Increasing the possibility of abuse is just one more devastating consequence of the frequent breakup of the nuclear family.

David Finkelhor, a major researcher on the subject of child sexual abuse, has isolated eight factors that, taken together, have a very high relationship to the likelihood of sexual abuse. If at least five of the conditions are present, perhaps a 66-percent chance exists that the child has been or will be victimized. Each additional factor above five increases the child's vulnerability by 10 to 20 percent. These factors are:

1. Living with a stepfather.
2. Living, at some time, without a natural mother. This could include living with a stepmother and father or only with a father.
3. Having a mother who is emotionally distant, often ill, or unaffectionate.
4. A mother who never finished high school.
5. A sexually punitive mother who scolded, warned, or punished for asking sexual questions or who was highly suspicious of even normal sexual behavior.
6. Little or no appropriate physical affection from the father, who is often characterized by an authoritarian personality that demands obedience from the child and submission from the wife.
7. Family income under $10,000 (1978 dollars).
8. A child who has only two friends or less in childhood, and tends to be a loner.[8]

This checklist is still in the process of refinement, so do *not* panic if your child or a child you know has at least five factors present in his or her life. But the research *is* strong enough to indicate you should investigate carefully. Be concerned for the child. He or she may be at risk. Material in the next chapters will tell you what to do if you suspect abuse.

Those who sexually abuse children tend to seek out victims who are easily controlled or manipulated. They are less likely to molest assertive youngsters who won't submit to their threats. Some characteristics of the more vulnerable child are these:

☐ Fearful to say no to adults or authority
☐ Fearful of punishment
☐ Fearful of being called "bad"; wants very much to please
☐ Insecure; low self-esteem; needs attention
☐ Strong desire for love and affection
☐ Physically or mentally disabled
☐ Left alone for long periods or with little supervision
☐ Naive about sexual matters; does not know about private parts or good and bad touches[9]

Children must be taught to respect authority, but they must also recognize adults are not *always* right. There is a very legitimate place to demonstrate courage and boldness when authority and power is misused (that's why Daniel ended up in the lion's den). Learning how to be assertive in appropriate ways is not something that comes naturally to most children. Assertiveness can become confused with a strong will, rebellion, and selfishness, but it is a quality that needs to be taught and practiced with our children.

CONSEQUENCES OF CHILD SEXUAL ABUSE

Most experts believe sexual abuse is nearly always a profoundly disruptive, disorienting, and destructive experience for the child. She has experienced a degree of stimulation that is far beyond her capacity to understand. This confusion interferes with the accomplishment of normal developmental tasks. The progression of mastery of one's self, environment, and relationship with others is significantly disrupted by the child's permanently altered awareness and new role with the perpetrator.

The child is frustrated by the contradictions she faces: "Is this man my lover or my father? Am I my mother's mother? How can I participate in this activity which keeps my family together, when

I feel wrong and the outside world believes it's wrong? How can I be loved yet avoid the sexual activity?"

The child has a secret she cannot share. This situation leads to feelings of alienation and separation from her family and friends. Though confusing, her special status may lead her to feel she has an inordinate sense of power. She may manifest this power via an air of superiority or haughtiness. Or she may perceive herself as having an evil power to corrupt or to contaminate.

Another result of her alienation may be self-blame, both for the event and for its consequences. Mixed with her guilt and her alienation is the compounding factor that, at some level, she has enjoyed the sexual experience. The longing to return to these experiences, at least in fantasy, can only intensify her ambivalence.

The sexually abused child is depreciated in value and becomes more of an object than a person. In cases of incest, she may feel burdened with the responsibility of holding the family together through her relationship with the perpetrator.

Child sexual abuse is disorienting because profound blurring of boundaries inevitably follows exploitation. A victim can't avoid questioning limits set for her and for others. She will be confused about the appropriate uses of power and authority. Her very identity is at stake when she asks herself, "Who am I, that I am both a child and a sexual partner of someone who is supposed to be parenting, nurturing, or protecting me?"

These dilemmas create guilt, shame, fear, and anxiety. For an estimated 20 percent of sexually abused victims, severe depression may follow and may be associated with suicide attempts. In 40 percent of the cases, problem behaviors develop, including irritability, school truancy, deteriorating classroom performance, health complaints, sexual promiscuity, running away from home, and lying. For another 20 percent, frigidity in adult life seems to be the consequence of this awkward initiation into adult sexuality. Probably only 20 percent come through the incest experience unscathed.[10]

Many sexually abused children have very poor self-images, possess inadequate social skills, and are reluctant to trust any other human being.

Many women who were abused as children describe serious difficulty in attaining a satisfactory level of emotional self-sufficiency or independence as adults. Nearly all attribute a lack of confidence to their childhood victimization. They may become dependent on drugs or alcohol, or become carbon copies of their mothers.

Two final consequences are particularly important. Childhood sexual victimization may increase the likelihood that an individual will become a perpetrator as an adolescent or adult. An extremely high percentage of convicted child abusers were themselves abused as children. This is another clear example of the sins of the fathers being passed on to the third and fourth generations. Abuse begets abuse.

Women who were sexually abused in childhood tend to select mates who, in turn are likely to abuse them and sexually exploit their children. While these mothers may not actually abuse their children, they are more likely to marry men who will. Either way, the children are made more vulnerable by the abuse inflicted on their parents as children.

Results of sexual abuse leave no doubt about its negative long-term effects. The erosion of self-esteem and the inability to trust are the major scars. What future is there for a child who hates herself and others?

SYMPTOMS OF CHILD SEXUAL ABUSE

Symptoms found in sexually abused children can be categorized in three ways: behavioral, medical, and familial. As is true of other lists of indicators relating to child maltreatment, most of the indicators are not, of themselves, absolute proof of sexual abuse. But if any obvious symptoms or several of the possible indicators are observed, an immediate attempt should be made to investigate further.

1. *Behavioral indicators.* A trauma such as child sexual abuse is certain to manifest itself. Usually no clear physical signs of abuse are apparent, so the child herself is the best and sometimes only source of warning signals. These behavioral signs will vary according to the age of the child. Keep in mind normal developmental milestones in applying these indicators to specific children.

☐ Indirect hints or open statements about abuse

27

☐ Difficulty in peer relationships, i.e. violence against younger children
☐ Withdrawn, less verbal, depressed, or apathetic
☐ Abrupt and drastic personality changes
☐ Self-mutilation
☐ Preoccupation with death, guilt, heaven, or hell
☐ Retreat to fantasy world, dissociative reactions—loss of memory, imaginary playmates, child uses more than one name
☐ Unexplained acquisition of toys, money, or clothes
☐ Fear, clinging to parent, requires reassurance
☐ Unwillingness to participate in physical/recreational activities
☐ Refusal to undress for PE class at school
☐ Sudden increase in modesty
☐ Fear of bathrooms and showers
☐ Self-conscious about use of bathroom, severe reaction if intruded upon
☐ Anger, acting out, disobedience
☐ Refusal to be left with potential offender or caretaker
☐ Becoming uncomfortable around persons he or she used to trust
☐ Active hostility and anger toward formerly trusted person
☐ Runaway behavior
☐ Refusal to go home or stated desire to live elsewhere
☐ Extreme fear or repulsion when touched by an adult of either sex
☐ Touching to either extreme
☐ Inappropriate dress, use of clothing to reverse roles—child looks like sophisticated adult, mother like teenager
☐ Onset of poor personal hygiene, attempts to look unattractive
☐ Sophisticated sexual knowledge
☐ Precocious, provocative sexual behavior
☐ Seductive, indiscriminate display of affection
☐ Pseudo maturity, acts like small parent
☐ Regression to earlier, infant behavior—bed-wetting, thumb-sucking

☐ Sleep disturbances, nightmares
☐ Sleep habits change—stays up late or seems constantly tired
☐ Continual, unexplained fear, anxiety, or panic
☐ Onset of eating disorders—anorexia, bulimia, compulsive eating
☐ Inability to concentrate in school, hyperactive
☐ Sudden drop in school performance
☐ Overly compliant or almost compulsive in action
☐ Arriving early at school and leaving late with few, if any, absences
☐ Excessive masturbation
☐ Combination of violence and sexuality in artwork, written schoolwork, language, and play
☐ Hysterical seizures
☐ Attempts to establish boundaries, such as wearing clothing to bed
☐ Total denial of problem with lack of expression or feeling

2. *Physical and medical indicators.* Some of the signs of abuse recorded in the following list can only be evaluated by a physician. Others can be observed by a parent or caretaker who has fairly close contact with the child. And a few symptoms can be observed by concerned persons such as the child's teachers. While sexual abuse often leaves no physical signs, if such symptoms *do* appear they represent some of the most conclusive evidence of abuse available. Immediate action should then be taken to prevent further injury or disease.

Even medical personnel have historically been uncomfortable in talking to a child about possible abuse. *Do not* make medical judgments unless you are qualified. *Do be* sensitive, calm, and reassuring in your questioning. Remember, the best source for discovering the cause of pain, swelling, or bruises is the child herself.

☐ Passive during pelvic examination—nonabused child is usually more agitated during first pelvic, raped child will yell and scream, repeatedly abused child will quietly spread legs

☐ Bruises and hickeys or both in the face or neck area or around the groin, buttocks, and inner thighs
☐ Torn, stained, or bloody underclothing
☐ Bleeding from external genitalia, vagina, or anal region
☐ Swollen or red cervix, vulva, or perineum
☐ Postive tests for gonococcus or spermatozoa
☐ Experiences pain or itching in genital area
☐ Difficulty in walking or sitting
☐ Has venereal disease or gonorrhea infections
☐ Pregnancy
☐ Unusual and/or offensive body odors
☐ Abrasions and erythema (redness) of the vulvar area, laceration of posterior fourchette
☐ Small perihymenal scars and scarring of posterior fourchette
☐ Abrasions and laceration of hymen with tearing between 3 o'clock and 9 o'clock
☐ Scarred and thickened transected hymen with rounded redundant hymenal remnants, with adhesions sometimes binding hymen laterally and distorting the opening
☐ Complete or partial loss of sphincter control
☐ Fan-shaped scarring extending out from anus in 6 o'clock position
☐ Pain on urination
☐ Penile swelling and penile discharge
☐ Vaginal discharge and urethral or lymph gland inflammation[11]

3. *Familial indicators.* The following symptoms are taken from the research on families where child sexual abuse has been found to occur. Not all abused children will have families with these particular features, but if a number of these signs are observed, the children should be considered at some level of risk. Use caution and good sense in any kind of intervention, but do not avoid taking action just because it is inconvenient or troublesome. Remember, the lives and health of possible victims are at stake.

Sibling Behavior

- [ ] A brother and sister who behave like a girlfriend and boyfriend
- [ ] Child fears being left alone with sibling
- [ ] Children appear to be embarrassed when found alone together
- [ ] Child is teased or antagonized by sibling but does not retaliate
- [ ] Siblings report another child is favored by parent

Parental Behavior

- [ ] Stepfather present in the home
- [ ] Parent, particularly the natural mother, absent from the home by death, divorce, long-term work, or military commitments
- [ ] Emotionally distant mother
- [ ] Sexually punitive mother
- [ ] Mother does not have high-school education
- [ ] Little or no appropriate physical affection from the father
- [ ] Strained marital relationship
- [ ] Dysfunctional family system, blurring of generational lines
- [ ] Parent often alone with one child; work or school schedules which cause one parent or caretaker, particularly the father or male family member, to spend great deal of time with a child
- [ ] Favoritism by parent toward one child
- [ ] Overly protective or jealous parent
- [ ] Reversal of roles between mother and daughter
- [ ] Parent severely restricts child's outside contacts with peers
- [ ] Mother chronically ill or disabled
- [ ] Questionable sleeping arrangements, often sleeping with one parent or exposure to parental sexual behavior
- [ ] Domineering, inflexible father won't allow wife to drive or interact with outsiders
- [ ] Father who either directs all family activities or sel-

31

dom participates in any family/social functions
☐ Strong parental reaction to sex-education activities at church or school
☐ Parent or other family member who has been sexually abused
☐ Social, physical, and geographic isolation of the family
☐ Overcrowding or substandard living conditions
☐ Existence of alcohol or substance abuse in the family[12]

Most of the time children do not clearly disclose their abuse. They drop hints. For example, the child may ask questions about men's underwear. If the parent responds with a comment that shames the child, the door is closed to further revelations.

Listen and observe carefully. Don't become paranoid and communicate fear and suspicion to the child. Instead look for danger signs and provide a safe and accepting atmosphere for the child to tell you what is going on in her world. More will be said about this in chapter 6.

Now we will turn our attention to the offender and the characteristics and qualities that typify the person who sexually abuses children.

NOTES

1. Julie Emery, "Rapes of Boys Are Increasing, Studies Show." *The Seattle Times*, Aug. 14, 1986, B6.
2. David Finkelhor, *Child Sexual Abuse* (New York: The Free Press), 1984, p. 166.
3. Ibid., p. 23.
4. Kathleen A. Kendall-Tackett, "Child Sexual Abuse from the Victim's Point of View: An Examination of Factors Affecting Treatment." Paper read at Western Psychological Association Convention, Seattle, May, 1986.
5. Diana E. Russell, "The Incidence of Prevalence of Intrafamilial and Extrafamilial Abuse of Female Children," *Child Abuse and Neglect,* vol. 7, no. 2, 1983, pp. 133-146.
6. Finkelhor, *Child Sexual Abuse,* p. 25.
7. Family Research Council of America, "Did You Know?",

Family Research Today, vol. 2, no. 4, July/August, 1986, p. 4.

8. Adapted from *Child Sexual Abuse*, pp. 25-29.
9. Adapted from Angela R. Carl, *Child Abuse! What You Can Do About It* (Cincinnati: Standard Publishing, 1985), p. 48.
10. Doris Sahd, "Psychological Assessment of Sexually Abusing Families and Treatment Implications," in *Sexual Abuse of Children: Implications for Treatment*, W.M. Holder, ed. (Englewood, Colo.: American Humane Association, 1980), p. 85.
11. Astrid Heger, "Pediatrician Describes Examination for Abuse," *American Medical News*, March 22, 1985, p. 14.
12. Some family indicators adapted from David B. Peters, *A Betrayal of Innocence* (Waco, Texas: Word, 1986), p. 103.

CHAPTER THREE

Who Makes the Children Cry?

Description of Offenders

"He who brings trouble on his family will inherit only wind"
(Proverbs 11:29).

Barbara had already experienced years of family violence by the time she was twelve. Her father had battered her mother practically from the day Barbara was born. But things looked like they were finally taking a turn for the better. Barbara's father had indicated a sincere desire to change his behavior and it appeared her parents were going to work things out.

To help get the reconciliation off to a good start, the three kids were sent off to relatives for a couple of weeks. Barbara went to her aunt's house in Montana. Her aunt had remarried a few months earlier, and the new uncle seemed nice.

After her return from Montana, Barbara's mother began noticing changes in her behavior. She was much moodier, spent most of the time in her room, and seemed extremely self-conscious about her body and personal hygiene. It took days to get to the source of the problem. But her mother persisted, and found the two weeks in Montana were ones of horrible sadistic sexual abuse by Barbara's uncle.

The discovery led to a formal investigation, criminal charges, more interviews, court testimony, cross-examination, and conviction of the uncle on numerous counts of rape and indecent liberties.

Barbara may remember with horror and pain those two weeks for the rest of her life. She was another victim of child sexual abuse by a trusted family member. This is the kind of trauma and sin which, according to Proverbs, shall result in an empty emotional and spiritual inheritance for the unrepentant offender.

As concerned parents or caretakers, we need to know as much as possible about the characteristics of child molesters and how they entice and seduce trusting children. If we understand how a person addicted to sexual behavior thinks and operates, we can do more in the way of prevention. We don't want to distrust every adult who is nice to children. But we do need to be informed, so we can pass on lessons of protection to those entrusted to our care.

WHY DO OFFENDERS ABUSE?

One of the issues in understanding sexual abusers is the question of whether or not sexual abuse is sexually motivated. Some researchers have suggested abuse comes from the need of the offender to gain power and control by hostile and aggressive means. Therefore child sexual abuse has been seen as a power problem more than using a child to fulfill sexual desires.

However, sex is always in the service of other needs. Even sex in marriage can be motivated by nonsexual needs such as a need for affection, a need to confirm one's masculinity or femininity, a need to affirm commitment, or a need to reduce stress. There is evidence that in much pedophilic behavior (sexual perversion in which children are the preferred sexual object) a strong erotic component is present, a component often strengthened by pornographic material and fantasy. Therefore, attempts to explain why people abuse children must include both sexual and nonsexual components.

There seem to be four preconditions that must be met before

sexual abuse occurs. *First,* the potential offender needs to have some sexual feelings toward a child. He must be motivated toward being sexual with children.

Offenders seem to fall into one of two categories. Some have a long-standing sexual preference for children. Emotionally and sexually, they identify with children, usually male, and in some ways want to remain children themselves. Often called *fixated* offenders, they tend to adapt their behavior to the level of the child in an effort to have the child accept them as an equal.

Regressed offenders, on the hand, revert to sexual encounters with children as a result of stress or conflict in their adult relationships. Usually married, they impulsively offend when crises arise in their lives. For the most part, these persons are sexually oriented toward adults and when they select a child as a substitute, they tend to relate to the child as if the child were their peer.[1]

This first precondition of motivation can also be influenced by the fact that alternative sources of sexual gratification are not available or are not satisfying. For example, the offender may feel his wife is unavailable and looks to a child as a substitute.

The *second* precondition for abuse is that the offender must overcome internal inhibitions against carrying out sexual behavior with a child. Essentially, the offender must overcome his conscience which says being sexual with children is wrong. Here is where rationalizations such as "I was just teaching the child about sex," "Children are supposed to obey their parents," or "I was under the influence of alcohol" are used by the offender to excuse his behavior.

Somehow, the abuser, if a Christian, has to ignore the exhortation given by the Apostle Paul, "Do not offer the parts of your body to sin, as instruments of wickedness, but rather offer yourselves to God" (Romans 6:13).

The *third* precondition is overcoming any external inhibitors such as the presence of other adults. If the child's mother is ill, for example, and unable to carry out her normal caretaker functions, the child is more vulnerable to abuse. This is not to put any blame whatsoever on the mother. It just points out how family members, neighbors, and even the child's friends all have a restraining influence on the actions of a potential abuser.

Living in isolated areas, unusual sleeping or living conditions, or even a mother who is dominated or abused by the father are other factors which seem to contribute to either the opportunity or interference of abuse with a child.

Children themselves play an important role in whether they are abused or not. The *fourth* precondition is overcoming the resistance of the child. Children have some capacity to avoid or resist abuse. Abusers can sense that a given child will not play along, will not keep the secret, will say no, or cannot be intimidated. This front of invulnerability is confirmed by molesters who have reported they know almost instinctively who is a promising target and who is not. Many children may have resisted abuse just by being themselves.

This precondition has important implications for prevention of abuse, and more will be said about that in chapter 6. For now, remember that the absence of a child's resistance or its being overcome in some fashion is the final prerequisite for the occurrence of sexual abuse.[2]

All four preconditions have to be met for sexual abuse to occur. The presence of only one condition, for example, an absent mother or inadequately supervised child, is not enough to explain the abuse.[3]

These preconditions work into a logical sequence. For a variety of reasons, some individuals have strong motivation to become sexually involved with children. Of those with this inclination, only some overcome their internal inhibitions and try to act on their motives. Of those who override their consciences, some will then have to overcome the surveillance of other family members or the lack of opportunity and plan ways to act on their impulses.

At this point, the potential abuser must overcome the resistance of the child. Then, one of three things will happen. The child will resist, knowingly or unknowingly, either by running away, saying no, or presenting an invulnerable demeanor.

A second outcome is that the child may fail to resist and be abused. Finally, a child may resist but have his or her resistance overcome by coercion or threat.

CHARACTERISTICS OF THE INCEST OFFENDER

Sexual offenders who are somehow related to their victims seem to be the most common type of abuser, particularly within the church community. Interestingly those who commit incest cannot be distinguished from those who do not on the basis of any major demographic characteristics. Such offenders do not differ significantly from the rest of the population in regard to level of education, occupation, race, religion, intelligence, or mental status. They come from all socioeconomic classes. They *do* differ from non-offenders in the fact that when faced with overwhelming life stressors, they seek relief from the situation through sexual activity with children.

The incest offender is usually an insecure and socially immature male. He does not have social skills for relating to adults, particularly in intimate situations. He has trouble sharing feelings because of both lack of personal awareness and lack of ability to express congruently how he feels. Some offenders appear to be comfortable with their peers in social settings, and may even have positions of leadership. However, they do lack the ability to satisfy their affection and attention needs through adults.

Incestuous fathers have been described as coming from all areas of society. The typical offender is intelligent, perceived by others to be a good provider, religious, and an active church attender. He has a poor self-concept and lacks full control of his impulses. He is socially isolated, feels needy and neglected, and lacks intimacy in his life. His marriage is not satisfying, and he was likely abused or emotionally neglected as a child.[4]

Like the Pharisees rebuked by Christ, many incest offenders have rigid beliefs and authoritarian manners. They want to be the head of the household and in control. For some, this is accompanied by strong, alleged religious beliefs which are very opinionated and divided into clear but simplistic compartments. Often the offender is extremely regular in church attendance, but has no sense of community or participation in the fellowship of the church.

Some of the basic problems for the incest offender are his inner feelings of helplessness, vulnerability, and dependency. As he tries to meet the daily stressors of marriage, parenthood, and vocation, his long-standing insecurities come to the surface. He feels overwhelmed and his usual coping mechanisms begin to fail him. As a result, he may use one of two responses to try to cope with his situation. First, he may withdraw from adult responsibilities and adopt a *passive-dependent* role within his family. By becoming dependent, the offender relinquishes control to the rest of the family and withdraws from the demands and responsibilities of his marriage. The incestuous relationship becomes his substitute for meeting needs of success and control.

The second possibility is to overcompensate by adopting an excessively rigid, controlling, *authoritarian* position. He becomes the family patriarch, often using Scripture and concepts such as submission and obedience to support his position. This position of dominance allows the offender to rule and control the rest of the family and reassures himself of his adequacy and effectiveness. Incestuous behavior becomes his precarious attempt to compensate for feelings of loss or inadequacy.

Like an alcoholic, the incestuous offender becomes dependent on sexual activity to meet his emotional needs. The sexual relationship is used to express a variety of unresolved problems that are not just sensual in nature. Rather, the incest is more directly related to issues of competency, adequacy, worth, recognition, validation, status, affiliation, and identity. Incest can be the sexual misuse of power.[5]

SEXUAL ADDICTION

A common definition of alcoholism or drug dependency is a pathological relationship with a mood-altering chemical. For the alcoholic, his relationship with alcohol becomes more important than family, friends, and work. This relationship grows to the place where alcohol is necessary to feel normal. But to feel "normal" is also to feel isolated and lonely, since the primary relationship he depends on to feel adequate is chemical, not human.

The same is true for sexual addiction. The addict substitutes a deviant relationship to sexual behavior for a healthy relationship with others. The sexual addict's connection with a mood-altering experience becomes the central focus of his life.

Sexual addiction begins with a delusional thought process rooted in the addict's belief system. These core beliefs about himself affect how the addict perceives reality.

Each of us has a belief system, consisting of all the assumptions, judgments, values, and misbeliefs that we hold to be true. It is our model of the world. On the basis of that belief system we make decisions, interpret other people's actions, make meaning out of daily experiences, direct our relationships, and establish priorities. Our belief system is the filter through which we make choices.

Scripture validates this concept when it says "For as [a man] thinketh in his heart, so is he" (Proverbs 23:7, KJV); "Do not conform any longer to the pattern of this world, but be transformed by the renewing of your mind" (Romans 12:2); and "I have written...to stimulate you to wholesome thinking" (2 Peter 3:1).

If our thinking is clear, our choices will be good. But the addict's belief system contains faulty and inaccurate ideas. The following core beliefs have been found to be almost universally present in the thought processes of addicts:

1. I am basically a bad, unworthy person.
2. No one would love me as I am.
3. My needs are never going to be met if I have to depend on others.
4. Sex is my most important need.[6]

These core beliefs lead the addict to other faulty thinking patterns which support the addictive cycle. The resulting sense of being out of control and powerless serves to strengthen the core beliefs. These intensified beliefs activate still more preoccupation with sex, and the addictive system becomes fully engaged. Sexual behavior is the only thing that makes his isolation bearable, so he hangs on to it with everything he has.[7]

An addictive experience progresses through a four-step cycle which intensifies with each repetition. The steps in the cycle are:

1. *Preoccupation.* This is the sexually obsessive filter used by the addict. His mind is completely engrossed with thoughts of sex, and every encounter is seen in a sexual light. People become objects to be scrutinized as this trancelike mental state creates an unquenchable search for sexual stimulation.

2. *Ritualization.* This is the addict's special routine leading up to the sexual behavior. Ritualization intensifies the preoccupation, triggering arousal and excitement. The rituals are as important as or sometimes more important than the sexual contact. One cannot be orgasmic all the time, so the search and suspense

absorb the addict's concentration and energy.

3. *Compulsive sexual behavior.* This is the actual sexual act—the goal of the preoccupation and ritualization. At this point, the addict is powerless to stop his behavior, in spite of any prior resolves. He has lost control over his sexual expression, which is why he can be classified as addicted.

4. *Despair.* The feeling of utter hopelessness an addict has about his behavior and his powerlessness is the low phase of the four-step cycle, and occurs after he has been compulsively sexual. The feeling includes the sense of failure for not keeping the resolutions to stop, along with hopelessness about ever being able to control the behavior. Self-pity and self-hatred may also be experienced, along with suicidal thoughts.

The sexual abuse cycle is self-perpetuating because the ever-ready preoccupation thoughts can be used to bring the addict out of the pit of despair. Each new repetition adds to the previous experiences and solidifies the cyclic nature of the addiction. As the struggle continues, the addict's life will start to disintegrate and become unmanageable. Within this addictive system, sexual experience becomes the reason for living, the addict's primary relationship. The phases of behavior which lead to an altered state of consciousness make normal sexual behavior tame by comparison. This is the energizing force within the addiction.[8]

Child sexual abuse is progressive. It usually starts with milder forms of molestation and extends to more extreme behaviors. One of the reasons for this is that addictive behavior almost always escalates to higher levels of need and intensity.

Sexual addiction operates at three levels. *Level One* contains behaviors which are rationalized as normal, acceptable, or tolerable, at least to the secular community. Examples include masturbation, pornography, strip shows, and prostitution. Also included would be sexual behavior in marriage when one partner sacrifices important parts of the total relationship in the service of sexual needs. Demanding sex three times a day in spite of the wife's desires would be an example.

Addicts seldom stay in Level One. Eventually they move on to the next level in order to maintain their "high."

Level Two extends to behaviors which are clearly victimizing and illegal. These have been called nuisance offenses and include exhibitionism, indecent phone calls, indecent liberties, and voyeurism. While illegal, the enforcement is variable. The fact that there are victims and sanctions contribute to the addictive process. In other words, doing something that is risky or that might involve arrest makes the activity more attractive.

Level Three behaviors have significant negative consequences for the victims and legal implications for the offender, and include incest, molestation, and rape. Participation at this level of behavior shows a severe progression of the addiction.[9]

DYNAMICS AND SEQUENCE OF SEXUAL ABUSE

Because of the addictive nature of the problem, sexual encounters between adults and children usually fall into a predictable pattern. This section will describe the typical sequence of events that typifies not only incest but nonfamilial abuse as well.

Sexual seduction of children usually occurs in six separate phases: engagement, sexual interaction, secrecy, disclosure, suppression, and repression or recovery.[10]

Engagement phase. Child sexual abuse is an intentional act. *There are no accidental molestations.* Ninety-nine percent of the time, the perpetrator knows the child, giving him built-in and ready access. The first requirement for sexual seduction is that the offender needs to be alone with the child. Though the circumstances of opportunity may be accidental on the first encounter, the perpetrator can be expected to *create* opportunities for private interaction with the child thereafter.

Often the adult is in a legitimate position of power over the child. He then uses that authority to engage the child in sexual activity. If not a relative, the offender may be someone within the child's daily sphere of activities, such as a baby-sitter, coach, teacher, or youth leader.

Inducement or grooming is usually done in a low-key, nonforcible fashion, possibly by presenting the activity as a game or something that is "special" and fun. This entails misrepresentation of moral standards, either verbally or implicity. The power and authority of the adult conveys to the child that the proposed behavior is acceptable. Often enticement, encouragement, or instruction is used as a ploy for participation. For example, "I'm going to teach you a special game that will be our secret," or, "Feel my penis. It is all right to touch it. It makes me feel good," or, "If you let me just lie here a while, I'll buy you something nice." The offender explains that what is important to him about the sexual relationship is that he feels special to the child and he wants the child to love and appreciate him.

Rewards or bribes may be offered. But more often than not, the opportunity to engage in activity with a favored person is sufficient incentive for the child to participate.

The second method used to gain sexual access to children is through force, including threats, intimidation, or physical duress. This technique is usually employed by the less skilled and tactful perpetrator. For example, an offender may tell a child to do what he says or he will beat the child or throw the child out of the home.

A client of mine was threatened at knifepoint by her abuser over the course of several weeks while forced to participate in disgusting and terrifying sexual acts. The molester resorted to violence and threats when his suggestive talk and enticements did not work.

The successful perpetrator will manage to be coercive in a subtle fashion. Threats are seldom used *if* the offender is skilled. Physical force is rarely used to engage a child in the normal intrafamily situation. However, when sexual abuse of a child occurs within the context of a violent family, implied force or threat of force is strong because the child has seen her mother beaten as a result of not pleasing her father or stepfather.[11]

Sexual interaction phase. This phase encompasses a progression of sexual activity—predictably from exposure to fondling to some form of penetration. Sexual activity between an adult and a child may range from exhibitionism to intercourse, often progressing through the entire spectrum of sexual behavior.

Secrecy phase. After the sexual behavior has taken place, maintaining secrecy is necessary, for the abuser certainly does not want to be caught and held responsible for the abuse. Secrecy eliminates accountability. Secrecy also enables the behavior to continue. The offender wants the child to be available for further exploitation. Therefore, he must persuade or pressure the child to keep the activity a secret.

The child usually does keep the secret. Some children never tell. Others keep the secret throughout their childhood and disclose the abuse many years later. There are several reasons for keeping the secret. The child may have been offered rewards. She may have enjoyed the activity and wanted the behavior to continue.

This premature introduction to sexuality by someone important to the child may feel good on several levels. It may provide pleasurable sexual stimulation, enhance her self-esteem, make her feel grown up, or give her a "special" relationship.

Threats may have also been used to reinforce secrecy. Threats may include: the prospect of anger by a third party ("If you tell Mommy, she'll be awfully mad!"); separation of the adult from the home ("If you tell anyone, Mommy may divorce me or I may be sent to jail."); separation of the child from the home ("If you tell anyone, they'll put you in a foster home."); self-harm by the offender ("If you tell anyone, I'll kill myself."); harm to someone else ("If you tell anybody, I'll hurt your sister or your dog."); violence against the child ("If you tell anybody, I'll hurt you or kill you.")

The secrecy phase can last for months or years, especially if it occurs within the family.

The sexual behavior progresses over time, usually in the direction of greater intimacy. As the child grows older, a parallel increase in the frequency of incestuous sexual activity may occur. Whenever the situation comes to the attention of outside professionals, it's unlikely to be the first and only incident of sexual activity for the child.[12]

Disclosure phase. There are two ways disclosure of child sexual abuse can occur.

ACCIDENTAL DISCLOSURE. None of the participants decided to tell. Instead, the secret was revealed because of observation by a third party, physical injury to the child, discovery of a sexually transmitted disease, pregnancy, or precocious sexual activity by the child which raised questions.

Accidental disclosure most often precipitates a crisis. Depending on the people involved, a state of chaos, high anxiety, hostility, and fear may predominate. In spite of the confusion and anxiety, there are several advantages in the crisis situation. First, it brings the situation out in the open so intervention and treatment can take place. Second, it takes the decision to tell off the child's shoulders.

PURPOSEFUL DISCLOSURE. In this type of disclosure, a participant consciously decides to tell an outsider. It is often the child who decides to reveal the secret. A young child may tell the secret to share an exciting or stimulating experience. An older child tells for different reasons. A youngster who used to regard her father as a warm and loving person may see him as a self-centered, controlling individual when she enters adolescence. In earlier years she would be totally preoccupied by his attention; as a young teen she is more interested in peers and group activities outside the family. Her father, however, limits her social activities and she rebels against his restrictions. As her frustration mounts, she may finally reveal the secret in order to gain more freedom.

Other reasons for telling might include fear of pregnancy or concern for a younger sister.

Whether accidental or purposeful, the family's reactions to disclosure will range from denial and hostility to protection and concern. The offender is likely to react with alarm and denial. The prospect of publicity, loss of status, and criminal charges will motivate him to protect himself.

After disclosure, the offender can be expected to exploit his power position to the fullest, while undermining the credibility of the victim's allegations.

Mothers of incest victims face many pressures. Some mothers may have been aware of the abuse, but did nothing about it. Now they have to deal with their guilt. Even if they were not knowingly involved, mothers of victims must face the consequences of siding with the child sooner or later. If the offender provides the primary means of economic and emotional support, this may be a very difficult choice. If the abuser has been violent toward the mother in the past, she will fear physical retribution along with everything else.

It's not unusual for mothers to collapse under these combined pressures, abandon responsibility, avoid decisions, and withdraw from the situation. This only serves to give the abuser more opportunity to exert control over the family.

Siblings of victims may react protectively and with concern, or they may react defensively. Children fear disruption of family life or separation from one of their parents, even if the situation has been traumatic. Fear of the unknown can lead them to attack the victim, even if they agreed with her need to disclose the abuse.

All family members can be expected to react to disclosure of abuse with the perspective of "How will these events affect me?"

Only those with ample strength and security can be expected to sustain continuing concern and support for the victim.[13]

Suppression phase. Following disclosure, the dynamics of most abuse cases tend to enter a suppression phase. Even if the abuser was from outside the home, the child's family is likely to react by trying to suppress publicity, information, and intervention. Such suppression can lead to minimization of the abuse, statements like, "It's nothing to worry about; she'll forget about it soon."

In the case of incest, the perpetrator can be expected to exploit his power by pressuring the child and any other family members who appear to be cooperating with outside authorities. He will attempt to undermine the child's credibility, perhaps by claiming her to be a pathological liar or crazy. He may cite prior school problems or difficulties with peers as evidence that the child is untrustworthy.

Feeling isolated, fearful, and guilty, the child may give in and withdraw the complaint or simply stop cooperating with the investigation. It is at this point that many children recant or deny their disclosure. The pressure is too great and they simply say, "None of it is true. I just made it up because I was mad."

Repression or recovery phase. Child sexual abuse can have one of two endings. If the suppression phase was successful, everything may return to "normal." The family system will lapse into its old habits; nothing will have changed. The abuse may even begin again, sometimes with a new victim, often a younger child in the family. This is known as *repression.*

The more desirable conclusion, of course, is *recovery.* The road to recovery is long and difficult. Treatment takes at least one year and frequently two or more. Despite its difficulty and cost, this is the outcome to which victims, their families, and involved professionals should be committed. Do not be lulled to inattention just because the crisis has died down. Work with all the appropriate agencies to make sure the cycle of abuse is stopped and that the child you care for gets the help he or she needs.

Release from the bondage of sexual addiction must start by reversing the feelings of alienation and self-hate that is central to the addiction. Offenders need to establish roots in a caring community. With proper support they can replace faulty beliefs about themselves with healthy ones.

The process must begin by acknowledging they are powerless

over their sexual behavior. Only then can they start rebuilding relationships and taking responsibility for their behavior.

The core beliefs of the sexual addict described earlier in this chapter can be replaced by these:

1. I am a worthwhile person deserving of pride.
2. I am loved and accepted by people who know me as I am.
3. My needs can be met by others if I let them know what I need.
4. Sex is but one expression of my need and concern for others.[14]

The Twelve Steps of Alcoholics Anonymous have been adapted for sexual addicts, many of whom have found them helpful in overcoming their problems. These steps as found in Patrick Carnes' book, *Out of the Shadows*, are included below.

If you wish to locate a Twelve Step group or other professional help, check with your local pastor, Christian counseling services, private counselors, community mental health centers, or Alcoholics Anonymous and Al-Anon programs. Specific groups for sexual addiction include Sexual Addicts Anonymous, Loveaholics Anonymous, Sexaholics Anonymous, and Sexual Abuse Anonymous.

One of the most successful treatment programs for both victims of abuse and sexual offenders is Parents United, based in San Jose, California; phone (408) 280-5055.

The Twelve Steps of Alcoholics Anonymous Adapted for Sexual Addicts

1. We admitted we were powerless over our sexual addiction—that our lives had become unmanageable.
2. We came to believe that a Power greater than ourselves could restore us to sanity.
3. We made a decision to turn our will and our lives over to the care of God as we understood Him.
4. We made a searching and fearless moral inventory of ourselves.
5. We admitted to God, to ourselves, and to another human being the exact nature of our wrongs.
6. We were entirely ready to have God remove all these defects of character.

7. We humbly asked Him to remove our shortcomings.
8. We made a list of all persons we had harmed, and became willing to make amends to them all.
9. We made direct amends to such people wherever possible, except when to do so would injure them or others.
10. We continued to take personal inventory and when we were wrong promptly admitted it.
11. We sought through prayer and meditation to improve our conscious contact with God as we understood Him, praying only for knowledge of His will for us and the power to carry that out.
12. Having had a spiritual awakening as the result of these steps, we tried to carry this message to others and to practice these principles in all our affairs.[15]

NOTES

1. A. Nicholas Groth,"The Incest Offender," in *Handbook of Clinical Intervention in Child Sexual Abuse*, Suzanne M. Sgroi, ed. (Lexington, Mass.: D.C. Heath & Co.), 1982, pp. 215-218.
2. David Finkelhor, *Child Sexual Abuse* (New York: The Free Press), 1984, pp. 54-61.
3. Ibid., pp. 61-62.
4. Richard E. Butman, "Hidden Victims: The Facts about Incest," *His Magazine*, April 1983, pp. 20-23.
5. Groth, "The Incest Offender," p. 225.
6. Patrick Carnes, *Out of the Shadows: Understanding Sexual Addiction* (Minneapolis: CompCare), 1983, pp. 4-6.
7. Ibid.
8. Ibid., pp. 11-16.
9. Ibid., pp. 54-55.
10. Suzanne M. Sgroi, *Handbook of Clinical Intervention in Child Sexual Abuse* (Lexington, Mass.: D.C. Heath & Co., 1982), pp. 12-27.
11. Ibid., pp. 13-14.
12. Ibid., pp. 10-12, 14-15.
13. Ibid., pp. 17-24.
14. Carnes, *Out of the Shadows*, p. 138.
15. Ibid., p. 137.

CHAPTER FOUR

Stopping the Tears

Crisis Help for the Sexually Abused Child

Marilee was a cheerful and active second-grader who usually liked school. Lately she seemed quiet and withdrawn. Even though the weather was mild, Marilee wore a heavy dark coat all day long. The teacher expressed her concerns to the principal, who had the school nurse talk to Marilee. After a reluctant beginning, Marilee told the nurse she was afraid to go home. Further questioning revealed her stepfather had been molesting her when he put her to bed several times a week. The nurse called Marilee's mother and asked her to come to school as soon as possible.

* * * * *

Sharon's fifteen-year-old daughter Rita disclosed her abuse Saturday morning. The two of them were arguing about what the curfew had been for the previous evening. Sharon had expressed concern about Rita getting home so late. In the course of the disagreement, Rita had said, "What do you think we were doing, having sex?" Before her mother could say anything, Rita added, "Well, it wouldn't be the first time. And besides, it wouldn't be any worse than what Dad has been doing to me since the seventh grade." Storming out of the room, Rita shouted, "So what do you think about that?" and slammed the door in front of her stunned mother.

Learning about the sexual abuse of your child can be one of the most painful events in the life of any parent. It may come without warning, like Rita's admission, or confirmed after weeks of suspicion and worry. Regardless of the circumstance, the manner in which a parent responds is a crucial component in the child's level of damage.

Hysteria, criticism, or denial will make a bad situation even worse. Support, comfort, and encouragement, along with a systematic plan, will ease the child's trauma and restore her confidence. A proper response by the parents can bring an end to the emotional damage imposed by the abuse and begin the healing process.

This chapter offers some specific guidelines for helping the child through the *initial* crisis of abuse. Some coping ideas for the parent as well as some *long-term* supportive suggestions will be described in chapter 5.

Six-year-old Bobby was absentmindedly stirring his ice cream around in the bowl when he looked up at his father and said, "I don't like Amy. She's mean." Startled from watching the 6 o'clock news, Dad was tempted to defend Amy because he had known her as a reliable baby-sitter for several years. Bobby could be very strong willed, so Dad knew there had been times of confrontation between the two. But Dad resisted his initial reaction and encouraged Bobby to tell him why he didn't like Amy anymore.

"I don't like her pretend games," Bobby explained.

"What is a pretend game?" Dad asked, his heart beating a little faster.

"It's when she does the doctor stuff. I don't like it," Bobby answered.

Bobby looked downcast. "She told me never to tell, 'cause you'd get real mad."

"Bobby, that's not true. I won't get angry. In fact, I'm

glad you are telling me these things. It's important for me to know about your unhappy feelings," Dad said reassuringly.

"Well, she touches my bottom and makes me touch hers, and says it's just like doctors and nurses do. But I think it's yucky."

Forcing back tears of rage and pain, Dad went on to ask Bobby more questions about the game the trusted baby-sitter had been using to molest his son. Calmly and softly, Dad asked when and where the activity took place. He used a matter-of-fact tone as best he could, so Bobby wouldn't get frightened or upset. Occasionally, Dad wrote down a few notes regarding specifics, but was careful not to let the writing interrupt the flow of the conversation.

A couple of times Dad had to go get a drink of water to calm himself down so he could continue the conversation. After getting as many details as possible, Dad explained to Bobby that what Amy had done was wrong. He gave Bobby a hug and told him it was good to tell Dad about what had happened. He further reassured Bobby by saying Amy would not be around anymore, and he didn't have to play the doctor game ever again.

Bobby seemed greatly relieved after the talk and even asked for another bowl of ice cream.

INITIAL CONSIDERATIONS
Pray. The very first thing shocked parents should do when they find their child may have been abused is to seek the wisdom and counsel of God. When we lack understanding we should "ask God, who gives generously to all without finding fault, and it will be given to [us]" (James 1:5). Christ Himself has promised to give us help for all of life's battles: "For I will give you words and wisdom that none of your adversaries will be able to resist or contradict" (Luke 21:15).

Few of us will make all of the right decisions or have exactly the proper words when confronted with a crisis such as trauma to our children. But we have God's promise that His wisdom is always greater than our own (1 Corinthians 1:25). Therefore, we should get down on our knees and seek His strength when we are troubled (James 5:13).

Please Don't Hurt Me

The following guidelines draw on the best professional knowledge available for dealing with child sexual abuse. However, no amount of human understanding will supersede the fervent prayer of a concerned mother and father on behalf of their child.

* * * * *

It is important to be aware of the following circumstances surrounding cases of child sexual abuse:

1. *Children are usually molested by people they know.* Ninety-five to 99 percent of the time, the molester holds a position of trust or familiarity with the child. The child will be confused, fearful, and perhaps even suspicious of the person to whom she discloses the abuse. She trusted the offender and he took advantage of that relationship, so why should anybody else be any different? Give the child the freedom to have doubts and confused feelings. Acknowledge the possibility she may not even be sure about trusting you, but continue to reassure her.

2. *Violent attack is uncommon.* Most of the time a child will have been seduced, deceived, or bribed into participation in sexual behavior. Some form of coercion and pressure is present by the very nature of the crime, but physical violence is infrequent. The child needs attention, but only rarely is the situation life-threatening.

3. *Children seldom lie about abuse.* In only 1 to 5 percent of the cases does a child fabricate stories about sexual indecencies. Even when a false report is made, it still generally indicates a serious problem. Children have been known to lie when it was opportunistic, when coached by a parent as part of a custody battle, when they have been previously abused by someone else but generalized to an innocent party, or when they have a serious emotional problem. In each of these situations, a problem exists and should be acknowledged and resolved.

We adults often don't want to believe children in sexual abuse incidents because the truth of their accusations forces us to deal with unpleasant realities. However, it is best to assume the child is telling the truth until it is proven otherwise. Restrain the natural reaction to prove the child wrong or to convince yourself it's all a result of an overactive imagination. If the child is able to give any specific details of the physical aspects of the abuse, you can be very sure it is true. Even if the details are missing, the situation warrants close investigation.

4. *Children may not tell you directly about the abuse.* Sometimes a direct disclosure will be made with very little inquiry by the parent. Most often, however, changes in the child's behavior will be the only clues that something is wrong. That is why the indicators listed in chapter 3 are useful. Familiarity with the normal behavior of your child allows you to be sensitive to subtle deviations. Once there are questions, you can look for the source.

5. *Sexual abuse is a crime.* Whatever the rationalizations given by the offender, child sexual abuse is wrong. Our society and cultures before us have deemed that sexual behavior with children is immoral. Because of the grave consequences to children, child abuse has been declared a crime. Under no circumstances should it be minimized or ignored. Immediate and lasting attention is needed. Do not be a party to sweeping it under the carpet.

As I've mentioned already, sexual abuse is progressive and continual. It generally does not stop unless drastic intervention is taken and the offender is treated for his addiction. Unfortunately, other children are often abused because the offender is confronted in private, denies the problem or swears he will never do it again, and is allowed to remain untreated. Not only does the damage already inflicted go unheeded, but the probability of more trauma persists when the offender is allowed to avoid accountability.

THINGS TO DO IMMEDIATELY

1. *Take the child to a private place and ask her to tell you what happened in her own words.* Go to a separate room if other children are present. Unplug the phone. Send siblings to the neighbor's house. Do whatever is necessary to create a quiet atmosphere without interruptions. In a matter-of-fact manner, ask the child to tell you what happened. Get the specifics of who, what, where, and when. Let her use her own words. Don't correct her, but be sure you know what she means. Use her terminology in further discussion. If the child uses a term such as *pee pee* to refer to her vagina, don't require her to use the anatomically correct words.

Listen carefully. Ask gentle questions. Avoid guilt-inducing questions such as, "Why didn't you tell me sooner?" The child may already feel guilty for not having told.

It may be a good idea to take notes, especially about specific times, places, and actions. But don't make the note-taking so conspicuous it distracts the child.

Be sensitive to the importance of touch at this point. Most children will need hugs, embraces, hand holding, or other appropriate forms of reassurance. But be aware that touch could also be confusing now, and a usually affectionate child may pull away. Give her freedom to do that. Don't force yourself on her, but don't hold back in an unnatural way.

2. *Don't panic.* Good luck! What parent isn't going to panic under such conditions? At least try to get things under control. The goal is to present a cool head and a loving heart. But grant yourself permission to have an adrenaline rush or two. Many mothers have reported a God-given calm, supportive manner while talking with their child about the abuse. Later they collapsed on the bed and cried for two hours. That's perfectly permissible.

Try not to lose sight of the child's needs in this situation. She needs calm support and reassurance. If you find your circuits are overloading, draw on the support of your spouse or a close friend. The goal is to minister to the child, not make her a victim of further confusion.

3. *Give reassurance. First,* convey to the child that she did well to tell you in spite of any threats by the offender. Let her know you understand how hard it was to say something bad about someone she liked.

Second, let the child clearly know you believe her. As mentioned before, children usually don't lie about sexual abuse. In the rare cases where doubt may be warranted, at least communicate you understand that she is probably feeling scared or confused. Do not criticize or belittle the child. If inconsistencies are apparent in her story, accept what you can and clear up the questionable parts later.

Third, convey to the child that you are sorry this happened. She needs to hear and see your grief, for most likely she has been carrying the pain for days or months. The calm support mentioned earlier does not preclude tears. The child needs real emotional bonding at this time, and tears can impart needed empathy.

Fourth, let the child know you will protect her. Assure her she will not have to see the offender again until the situation is resolved. Don't make promises you can't keep. The child has had a trust violated. She doesn't need any more broken promises.

Fifth, acknowledge that what the offender did was wrong. At some level, the child knows something was wrong with what she was asked to do or with what was done to her. This sense of wrongness needs validated. Be careful to point out it was the offender who was wrong. The child was not to blame for what happened. Most victims assume the guilt for their abuse and for the crisis that results from their disclosure. Do all you can to alleviate this false guilt.

Emphasize that the fault lies with the offender, but do not threaten such measures as putting him in jail. That can just add to the child's sense of guilt for telling. A better response would be, "What Uncle Jim did was very wrong. It hurt you a great deal. Now we are going to do everything we can to get him some help so he doesn't hurt you or anyone else again."

4. *Make sure the child is safe.* Take immediate action to ensure the safety of the child. If the offender lives in the home, a difficult decision is necessary. It is usually far better for the offender, not the child, to leave home. The sense of abandonment and guilt is greater if the victim has to be dislodged. If there is any doubt about the child's safety, do not confront the offender with your knowledge of the abuse until the safety concerns are satisfied. The safety issue, when the offender is at home, is closely tied to the reporting decisions to be described shortly.

5. *Be prepared to submit the child to a medical exam.* If you suspect injury, have the child examined by a physician. Often disclosure does not occur immediately following the abusive incident. However, a medical examination is advised as soon as possible. Select a physician with whom the child will feel most comfortable. This may be her regular doctor, but be sure the physician is experienced in examining sexually abused victims. The increased awareness of child sexual abuse has improved the degree of sophistication in both the physical exam and in relating to the child's feelings. Select a trained and sensitive specialist.

If you have questions, call your local sexual assault or rape relief center for information and guidance.

A sensitive examination will be nonthreatening as well as

provide the child reassurance she has not been seriously harmed. If physical damage has occurred, a realistic appraisal is equally important so that appropriate treatment can be given.

If disclosure occurs immediately after the abusive incident, do not clean up the child or change her clothes. As hard as it may be to do, take the child the way she is. It is in the child's best interests for the medical personnel to have access to all the evidence of the abuse.

If you take your child to a medical facility, don't be afraid to remain in charge of your child's care. Advise the staff of the reason for your visit. Request that the police be notified of the situation. Once medical personnel are involved in an abuse case, by law it has to be reported. But don't assume it will be reported at that time. You want the medical staff and police to cooperate in the gathering of evidence. Blood and semen samples should be taken and clothing retained as evidence. Therefore, remember to bring a change of clothing for the child to wear after the examination.

Request that as few people as possible interview your child, and ask that a specially trained officer, preferably the same sex as your child, be made available. You know your child better than anyone else; guide the process in her best interests.

This is a traumatic time for everyone, but an important role for you as parent is to coordinate the various people or agencies who have contact with your child. If both parents, or you and a friend, are present, one of you should act as secretary. Ask questions about what is going on and write down the answers. Get the names of the police officers, caseworkers, nurses, and doctors involved. For a variety of legal and medical reasons, you may need to speak to some of these people again, and it will be a lot easier if you have good records.

Excessive repetition of interviews and examinations can be reduced if you know who has seen the child and are able to refer inquiries to the proper person.

During the entire examination and questioning process, try to stay with your child. Unless you become too distraught, your presence will be most comforting. However, sometimes authorities want a chance to talk to the child without the parents present. This can be appropriate, but if you find the process begins to focus too much on the needs and preferences of adults and not enough on your child, don't hesitate to intervene. You can't stop an uncaring doctor or policeman from further traumatizing your child if you are pacing the floor in the waiting room. Remember, you are the one ultimately responsible for the welfare of your child!

6. *Be careful about confrontation.* If the child was abused by a staff member from a school, day-care center, or church, be cautious about going directly to the administrators of those programs. Unless you are confident of the integrity of the person in charge, it is probably best to report the abuse to the proper investigative authorities. Too often a child's statements have been taken to church, school, or other authorities only to be whitewashed. The result is that the offender is not held accountable for his problem.

Many parents, motivated by outrage, disbelief, or fear of making a false report, want to confront the accused offender before making a report. Most of the time this is not a good idea. Sexual addicts can be very convincing and will probably deny everything. Call the appropriate agencies. All you need to make a report is your child's story. Let the professionals do the investigating.

7. *Initiate a report.* The decision to report an incidence of child abuse to Child Protective Services or the police is a difficult one to make. There is no question that the reporting, documentation, questioning, and environmental changes are disruptive and can throw the entire family into shock. The social, medical, and legal systems are unpredictable—sometimes sensitive, sometimes unfeeling—but more and more often, competent and caring professionals are available to deal with your child's trauma.

There are at least three considerations to evaluate in deciding whether or not to file a report: (1) protecting your child from further abuse, (2) helping your child recover from the effects of the assault, and (3) protecting other children from being abused by the offender.

It seems the criminal justice system is more concerned nowadays with protecting the rights of the accused than with meeting the needs of victims of abuse. You will need to investigate the social and legal services in your community to determine what is best for your child.

The decision can be more difficult when the perpetrator is a friend, a well-known member of the community, or a family member. Remember, the total responsibility for the abuse lies with the offender. You do not share in that responsibility, even if by reporting it you disrupt the abuser's family.

Most children can be involved in the decision. Ask your child how she feels about reporting the abuser in those cases when there is a choice. Most children want to help the offender get help and keep other children from being abused. Your child is probably not the first or last child to be abused by this person. Some types of adult offenders have sexually abused thirty to forty children by the time they are convicted.[1] Someone must take the initiative to put the indiscretions to an end.

If you should choose to consult with someone prior to making an official report, it is important to understand the mandatory reporting law. In all fifty states, professionals such as teachers, doctors, nurses, counselors, social workers, and sometimes pastors are required by law to report all suspected cases of child abuse and neglect. This means almost any professional person with whom you consult is bound by law to make a report. Parents who were not aware of this requirement have been devastated by an unexpected investigation.

Generally, my advice is to not keep secrets. Some kind of action is necessary. It may take much prayer and discernment to decide exactly what to do, but don't be lulled into doing nothing.

If a report is made, try to keep in control of the process. Keep your child informed about what is happening and involve her in as many decisions as is appropriate. It does no good to keep her in the dark.

Do not assume everyone is equally well trained to handle your child with sensitivity and competency. Seek out the best qualified people in the field. If you are not satisfied with the services, go to the next higher level. Be courteous and tactful, but assertive. Your child has already been abused by emotional incompetence; she doesn't need to be submitted to professional incompetence as well.

Children will often be interviewed repeatedly. You have the right to question this process. Request that the interviews be consolidated, taped, or whatever else is necessary to prevent the revictimization of your child.

If court testimony is necessary, make sure your child is adequately informed and prepared. She needs to know what kind of questions will be asked, the procedures used, the nature of cross-examination, and that the accused offender will be present. Some states have hearsay laws which allow testimony of persons to whom the child has disclosed the story to testify in court instead of the child. Find out the laws in your state.

Sex abusers have historically had one of the lowest conviction rates of any crime. One study revealed that only one in every sixty reported cases of sexual abuse resulted in conviction.[2]

These figures are changing, and the goal is more toward rehabilitation and treatment of the perpetrator than incarceration. Still, the ever-present reality is that sometimes very little good comes out of the legal process from the victim's viewpoint.

8. *Don't blame yourself.* There are two reasons for this recommendation. First, it doesn't do any good. Your child needs you at your fullest capabilities, not having a pity party. Second, self-blame is not appropriate because the offender committed the crime, not you. Guilt is true only when there are responsibility and accountability for actions. As a conscientious parent you had no idea your child was in danger. If lessons can be learned from the situation, apply them and move on. But don't blame yourself.

9. *Draw on your support system.* The child needs support and reassurance during this time of crisis, and so do you. Don't try to undertake the whole emotional load. Seek out those who love and care for you. For many, this will be a husband or wife. For some, it will include friends or extended family. Your child doesn't need you around every minute, so take some time to recharge the batteries. Let your Bible study- or prayer group know something of what is going on, so they can pray and support you.

Your local rape relief center may be able to direct you to support services and personnel if you need someone outside your immediate circle of family or friends.

10. *Watch out for crisis vulnerabilities.* When some people experience a crisis, they eat too much. Others drink, sleep, talk, or indulge in something to excess. Know yourself. If you have certain vulnerable points that show themselves in times of crisis, take preventative action. You don't want to get your child safely through the next couple of months, only to have yourself crash and burn because you've gained thirty pounds!

If you have identified a routine that helps you cope with a

crisis, now is the time to use it. This may be a good time to start keeping a journal or diary of the events and your feelings. Prayer will continue to be important. Again, don't try to do it all yourself.

Sexual abuse of children is a serious and tragic event. It should not be ignored. Above all, take action to ensure the safety of your child as well as the safety of others who might be abused if no action is taken. Be prayerful, but diligent; discerning, but direct. Now is the time for a tough love for the offender and compassionate love for the victim.

This chapter has dealt with the initial decisions and events following disclosure of sexual abuse. The next chapter will focus on the needs of both the victim and parents in the period of recovery following the disclosure.

NOTES

1. A. Nicholas Groth, R. Longo, and J. McFadin, "Undetected Recidivism among Rapists and Child Molesters," in *Crime and Delinquency,* vol. 28, 1982, pp. 450-458.
2. Richard Devine, "Some Violence Statistics," *American Psychological Monitor,* February, 1978.

CHAPTER FIVE

Restoring the Joy

Follow-up Help for the Sexually Abused Child

In the days following Terrie's disclosure of her abuse by her uncle, my life seemed like a slow-motion movie. It felt like a dream. I went through the motions of living, but I had no feelings. My senses were dull; nothing seemed real. It was like watching it all happen to somebody else. Decisions were difficult. Then one day Terrie spilled a glass of milk and I screamed at her like I have never done before. She looked at me in terror and I realized what I had done. I ran to the bedroom and cried for several hours. I don't know what happened, but when I got up I felt more alert and aware.

* * * * *

I was so mad at him. How could he do this to my little girl? Why would he betray me like this? Then I was angry at my daughter, Lucy. Why didn't she tell me? I could have stopped it. Why did she tell her teacher first? Doesn't she trust me? How could God ever let this happen? Question after question. Will I ever find the answers?

* * * * *

I sat down and thought about the implications of all of this. Then I felt really scared. My husband was in jail. There were going to be more bills for the attorney and counselors and we were already in debt. I wasn't sure I could ever bring myself to be around him again. How could we survive on just what I earn? Would Julie be all right? I was afraid she would never be normal again.

These are just some of the thoughts and feelings experienced by parents in the days following discovery of their child's molestation. Anger, fear, doubt, suspicion, anxiety, and guilt are all possible reactions. Then there are the details of picking up the pieces. Arranging for counseling, interviews with detectives, and decisions about living arrangements are only a few of the items that demand attention in the weeks following disclosure. This chapter gives some guidelines for helping to make that period a time of recovery rather than further disintegration.

DEALING WITH YOUR FEELINGS AS A PARENT
When a child is molested by a person outside the family, the reaction of parents is likely to be much better than when it involves abuse by a family member. When the abuser is a stranger, or even a teacher or coach, the parents are more likely to be supportive. The family usually draws together and targets their feelings on the outside offender. The emotional impact on the victim is minimized by the common bond of the family.

In cases of incest, there is almost always more confusion, division, and possible harm to the victim. When a mother learns her husband has abused the child, so many conflicting feelings emerge it makes it difficult to give proper support to the child. The mother wants to believe her child, but doesn't know what to do with her husband's intense denial. If she acknowledges the guilt of her spouse, the implications make her angry, disgusted, and guilty. Could she have prevented the abuse by being a better wife? Now she has to choose between sending her daughter to a foster home or making her husband leave. She is angry about having to choose between two people she loves.

62

If your child has experienced incestuous abuse, these intense and conflicting feelings can lead to outbursts toward your child which will further damage her. Regardless of the circumstances, you must not take your anger out on your child. To do so intensifies her anguish and can lead to anger and hatred toward both parents. Here are some feelings and reactions common to parents in the weeks following the discovery that their child has been abused. Knowing about the predictability of these reactions will help moderate their influence.

> *Numbness.* Emotional and physical sensations are in a state of shock, resulting in the inability to feel. Your sense of time is confused, and events seem to run together. This is part of the body's defense system to a crisis and will probably last only a few days.
>
> *Distance.* This is a feeling of being detached from other people and events, often reported as watching yourself in a slow-motion movie. This is usually another part of the initial reaction to stress. It can be a way of standing back and evaluating what has happened. A feeling of separation can keep the circuits from overloading and give you time to process the trauma.
>
> *Disbelief.* Daily life doesn't seem real. You may keep telling yourself the whole thing is simply a bad dream. Recall and memory are diminished. Your system doesn't want to deal with the trauma. A sense of reality eventually will take over, but the transition may be quite emotional.
>
> *Anger.* Often this anger is generalized, particularly if the abuse was incestuous. You feel mad at everyone—the abuser, the victim, the church, CPS workers, the police, and yourself. Anger can be very appropriate, but try to channel it toward the right source and use its energy to motivate you into correct action. Talking to a counselor or pastor may be very helpful here.
>
> *Guilt.* Feelings of self-blame are almost guaranteed, at least for a while. You believe the abuse was your fault. You could have prevented it if only . . . ; you should have been able to see it coming; etc. The responsibility here is the offender's. You did not abuse your child and do not deserve the guilt.

Betrayal. You may feel hurt because your husband looked to your daughter for sexual needs and not to you. You may feel pain because you have assumed he did this to hurt you. The secrecy and lies that accompanied the abuse are difficult to handle. Likely the offender was out of control and power-less to cope with his addiction. He probably did not intend to hurt you or the victim, even though he must be accountable for his actions.

Jealousy. Sometimes mothers of victims feel jealous of the relationship that developed between their child and husband. You may believe your own lack of sexual attrac-tiveness drove your partner to seek out your child. Or you may think your child had some special qualities that were attractive to your husband which you do not have. The truth is, the offender took advantage of a child's trust and lack of power, and used that situation to meet his own need. That is not something for which you should be jealous. Your sexual qualities were not a factor in his decision to molest.

Spiritual doubt. You may be asking what sin God is punishing you for to allow this thing to happen. You will wonder why God would allow a helpless child to be abused. What kind of testing is this and how can God possibly use it for any good cause? These questions are natural yet difficult to answer. Don't feel guilty because you have asked them. God has promised to be faithful in all things (Isaiah 43:2; 2 Thessalonians 3:3). Talk to someone about your doubts and fears. Sharing your feelings is an important part of the healing process.

Minimizing. One of the grave dangers is to tell yourself the situation is really not that serious. It's tempting to believe the offender's story that it only happened once, or that it only involved an accidental touch. Or you may want to believe the impact on your child is slight and that the offender will be able to correct things and life can go on pretty much as before. The reality is that this is a serious event. Your child has been traumatized and it will take significant intervention to correct. Therapy often lasts two years. The family will undergo long-term changes. You cannot just forgive and forget. The sin that led to the abuse must be corrected.

Fear, confusion, and worry. Worry over financial obstacles, what will happen if you separate, or if your husband will lose his job will be common concerns. What will the people in the church and community think? Confusion over who to tell, what to say, or whether you have the ability to make good decisions under the circumstances are all possible sources of discouragement. A support group of friends, family, pastor, or counselor is important to lean on at this point. The next few months will be very confusing, and you will need help in sorting through your alternatives. Don't try to carry the load by yourself.[1]

Many other feelings can be experienced during the months following the disclosure of abuse. But these will give you an idea of the normalcy of your own experience. Don't try to deny or avoid these reactions. Work them through with a friend or counselor, and be steadfast in prayer. The crisis stage will pass. Eventually a plan will emerge that will prove helpful to all those who want the help and who are willing to make the appropriate changes.

HELPING YOUR CHILD AFTER INITIAL DISCLOSURE

1. *Continue to believe your child.* Continued support is one of the most important considerations in the weeks following the discovery of abuse. Do not convey anything that would imply the child is to blame. Statements like, "If this had never happened, we would have money to buy you a new dress," should be avoided. I'm not suggesting you shouldn't talk about the situation, but do not cast doubt on your child.

Continued belief in your child can be very difficult when the offender continues to insist the abuse never took place. It is easy for a parent to become so overwhelmed with anger and frustration that she strikes out at her child. Take advantage of the professionals involved in the case. Express your hesitancy and doubt to the child's caseworker or counselor. Chances are one of them will be able to verify the truth of the child's accusations. Most of all, don't make your child a victim twice over by taking your feelings out on her.

2. *Consult with your physician regarding the need for continu-*

ing medical care. A victim of sexual abuse feels damaged by his or her experiences. If physical injury or pain occurred, the child has factual reason to believe she was damaged. Usually there is no physical impairment, but if a child experienced pain, it is understandable she would expect some kind of permanent damage.

Adolescent girls often ask, "Will I be normal when I grow up? If I have a baby, will it be all right?" If a victim has become pregnant, the experience provides concrete evidence of the trauma.

Treatment of the "damaged goods" syndrome should begin with a comprehensive physical examination of the victim, done by a physician who is knowledgeable about child sexual abuse. If physical damage did occur, it can then be treated. If no physical damage resulted, this fact should be conveyed to the victim and her family. The ability to state authoritatively that physical damage is absent or has been treated is a stepping-stone to convincing the victim she has not been otherwise damaged.

3. *Ensure continued protection from further abuse.* Take whatever steps are necessary to make sure your child is safe. In the case of incest, see to it the offender is removed from the home and not your child. Removal of the victim is usually perceived as punishment and makes her seem the source of the problem. Very often, when the victim is removed, it allows the molester to increase the pressure on the mother to believe his denial. This usually results in a division between the mother and daughter. One of the best ingredients in the recovery process is a strong and positive bond between mother and daughter. If this relationship is sabotaged, the chances for healing and reconciliation are greatly reduced.

If the offender is still at home, take maximum precautions that your child is never alone with him. Request your child to tell you immediately if any other sexual attempts are made, and instruct her on what to do if one is made. This is not an issue to be taken lightly.

My concern is supported by a study which found that 85 percent of the parents of children abused by strangers took immediate action to protect their children from further abuse. In contrast, only 60 percent of the parents of incestuously abused children took protective action. This same study found that 90 percent of the incest victims had been abused on more than one occasion. Only 27 percent of those molested by persons outside of the family had experienced multiple abuse.[2]

Be firm. Do not allow yourself to be manipulated by the offender into taking any chances with your child. Precautions must be consistently enforced. Brothers and sisters must also be protected, as an abuser will often molest another child in the family when he no longer has access to the initial victim.

4. *Continue giving reassurance and support.* Your child will need ongoing affirmation that the abuse was not her fault, nor does it make her a bad person. Intense feelings of guilt following disclosure of sexual abuse is almost universal. There are often three levels of that guilt.

RESPONSIBILITY FOR THE SEXUAL BEHAVIOR. Many children feel they are responsible for the sexual activity that took place as soon as they perceive society's response to their involvement.

RESPONSIBILITY FOR DISCLOSURE. When the secret is told by the child, she is obviously responsible for the disclosure. She may also assume responsibility when the disclosure was accidental or when someone else told. Under any circumstance, the child may feel she has betrayed the perpetrator.

RESPONSIBILITY FOR DISRUPTION. Disclosure of abuse leads to profound disruption for the victim and everyone around her. If the molestation is incest, the uproar is even greater. When the child tells her secret, she can be expected to feel guilty about the changes that result. Usually the disruption is greater than she expected. Even when problems flare up weeks or months later, the child may take the blame and feel guilty.

Help your child identify and sort out her guilt feelings. Then consistently convey to the child, other family members, and the perpetrator that your child can never be held responsible for initiating sexual activity with an older person. You can also tell the child she had a right to expect protection from the offender, and that she had a right to disclose the secret. The perpetrator is the one responsible for the sexual activity, including the disruption that followed. The victim should be praised for her courage and assured her confession will help the whole family in the long run.

Sometimes older children will have taken advantage of the favored position with the offender. They may have acted inappropriately toward their brothers and sisters. They may have become very manipulative or disobedient toward the non-offending parent or other family members. Such youngsters may experience some appropriate guilt for their conduct, and you need to help them sort through the distinctions. If there is legitimate guilt, the child should be helped to work through it and redirect her behavior.

5. *Respond to the child's questions.* Allow your child to talk about the situation any time she desires. Try to respond to her questions or feelings with a calm, matter-of-fact attitude. Do not pressure her by probing or prying for details.

I also tell parents of abused children to watch out for the rebound affect. This is how it often works. During a counseling session with an abused child, I may stir up some feelings or memories. The child may not tell me everything at that moment. But often, if the parents have been providing a safe and accepting environment, the child may say something on the way home from counseling or at another time. With younger children particularly, these are like little windows of opportunity.

For example, during counseling I may have introduced the subject of feeling afraid. I may also tell about another child victim who was afraid of future incidents of abuse as well as of retaliation. One of the ways fear shows itself is by nightmares or dreams. When asked about dreams at that moment, the child may tell me she hasn't had any nightmares. However, the next evening while being tucked into bed the child tells her mother about being afraid to go to sleep "because the monster with the big hands will get me."

This is the window of opportunity for parents. Help the child identify and determine the reality of her fears. Encourage her to express the feelings associated with her fears. Talk about God's protection, but remember the victim's experience to this point has seemingly been contrary to Scripture's teaching. Assure her that her living situation is being made as safe as possible and that steps are being taken to build trusting and safe relationships within and outside the family.

Don't tell the child to forget about the molestation. She needs to talk about her feelings. Questions are part of the grief process involved in losing a trust relationship. The more a child can talk about the experience, the more control she will gain over it. If she senses you are uncomfortable talking about the event, she will hold back, and the recovery process will be impeded.

If you can't remain reasonably calm while dealing with your child, this is a major sign you still need support.

6. *Respect the child's privacy.* Don't tell too many people about what happened. When the family and community learn the child has been prematurely introduced to sexual activity, it contributes to her perception that she has been mysteriously altered by the experience. The youngster is likely to be viewed with intense curiosity, pity, disgust, or hostility by those who know too many of the details.

Parents, siblings, teachers, and others should be made aware of how important it is *not* to treat the child differently from other children. The victim needs to be viewed as a child and not as an adult or a sexually sophisticated child.

If there is any risk for brothers or sisters of the victim, or for children in the neighborhood, they should be informed. But do not give the details of the abuse to anyone who doesn't need to know. It would be devastating to have the victim taunted or teased with specifics of the abuse by insensitive siblings or playmates.

On the other hand, the abuse should not be kept as a family secret. Don't contribute to the abuser's denial by pretending nothing happened. Proposing to tell an appropriate person can also give an opportunity to see how the child is feeling. If the child says, "Oh, no, don't tell Grandma, she won't love me anymore," it is a definite indication more reassurance is needed.

7. *Follow a regular routine.* Don't relax the expectations or responsibilities for your child. Encourage the resumption of a normal lifestyle as soon as possible. The longer normal activities are avoided, the harder it will be to take them up later. For example, your child may want to stay home from school for a time right after the disclosure. Like any other illness or trauma, a time of rest and recovery is appropriate. But if more than two weeks passes and the child still refuses to go to school, she needs professional help.

Other examples of disrupting the routine include delaying bedtime or desiring to sleep with you instead of staying in her own room. The child may not want to do her chores or continue his paper route.

8. *Monitor your own feelings and needs.* Sexual assault is very disruptive. Parents of victims will continue to need support. It is

crucial to be able to unburden yourself of the feelings of guilt, anger, and grief—for your own sake as well as for your child's. Tears and times of sadness or dismay are to be expected, but use a counselor or friend for your exploration, not your child.

If you were abused as a youngster, the disclosure of your child's sexual abuse may surface all the feelings and memories of your own molestation. Now may be an opportunity to talk to someone about your incident of incest or other sexual assault. This time of personal exploration may be an essential prerequisite to facing the realities of your child's abuse. The material on adults abused as children in chapters 7 and 8 would be appropriate for you to read at this point.

Some mothers want to know the details of their child's molestation, including what happened and when. If a report is filed, these details will emerge. Don't take it on yourself to uncover the specifics. Be available to your child's desire to talk about her feelings, but don't cross-examine.

Talk with other parents who have experienced child sexual abuse in their families. Ask your counselor, caseworker, sexual assault center, or child protective agency for information on mothers' or parent support groups.

In the days after learning of your child's molestation, expect a flood of memories to come over you. These memories can include clues of past months that you never quite pieced together. They can include subtle messages given by either your child or the offender that you never understood. This process may continue for some time as more details are revealed and more events are recalled. Sometimes these recollections will occur in the most unexpected places—in church, at the grocery store, while making your child's bed. These memories will trigger more expressions of anger, guilt, and hurt. Anticipate these times and draw on your support system to help you process each event. Recall can be painful, but is also part of the understanding that contributes to your ability to cope.

One of the biggest needs expressed by mothers of incest victims is how to regain control of their own lives and minds, including how to cope with day-to-day events and decision-making. It may seem like your life is a runaway locomotive, and you have no way to steer or put on the brakes.

Knowledge is the best form of regaining control. Start with

what you need to know in order to survive. How to report the abuse, how to keep up with the legal process, being aware of the services available to you and your child, and how to parent an abused child are some of the key things you need to know. This book and other local resources can start you on your way to adequately dealing with the trauma of abuse.

Other types of knowledge include how to make basic life decisions. What do you do about your marriage—separate, move away? How will you survive economically—get a job, sell the house, or go to school? Making a decision about how and whether to continue a relationship with the person who molested your child is one of the hardest. If the offender is your husband, many different aspects enter into the process. A few of the considerations mentioned by many mothers of incest victims include: whether or not you love him, if you think you can ever learn to trust him again, your belief about divorce, the financial considerations involved if he goes to jail or if separated or divorced, his willingness to get counseling and make efforts to change, and his feelings about you and the victim.

Most mothers need time and personal counseling to make permanent decisions about the marriage relationship. Immediate separation for the safety of the child is necessary. But the separation also gives you time to gain perspective on what has happened and to establish a stronger bond with the victimized child.

If your child is placed in foster care because of the abuse, you need to know your rights and options regarding custody. Don't sign anything without a full understanding of the document. Consult an attorney or at least ask the authorities for copies of the state regulations that relate to your situation.

It may be helpful to keep a journal of your feelings and thoughts for the weeks following the disclosure. Many people have found the mechanics of writing down their thoughts helped give perspective and insight that were missing when they merely "thought" about their situation. It also can be encouraging several months later to go back and see how the feelings have changed from those first desperate days, when panic and helplessness were dominant.

One of the constant recommendations for parents dealing with child sexual abuse is to find and maintain a support system. Your support system should include caring people with whom you can share all of your feelings and thoughts about the abuse and related issues. Sharing these intimate matters may be difficult, but the support will be very helpful in overcoming the loneliness, gaining encouragement, and feeling more confident.

Sources include your family, Bible studies, women's groups from church, sexual assault centers, or groups your pastor or counselor might recommend.

At times the trauma of abuse seems overwhelming. The following words by Ken Medema from his song, *Lord of the Troubled Sea*, express the plight, yet hope of the hurting Christian.

> Lord of the troubled sea, when I'm walking
> through deep water,
> You alone can be dry land beneath my feet.
> Lord of the flames, when I'm walking through the fire,
> You alone can shield me from the heat.
> Lord of the desert, when I walk across the burning sand,
> My mouth with living water You can fill.
> Lord of the storms, when the winds would
> tear my moorings loose,
> You alone are my word, "Peace, be still."
> That's why I say You are my all in all.
> You're the air I breathe, the song I sing, the help I call.
> And when I know I just can't cope, You alone
> are all my hope,
> For Your grace is enough for me.
> Lord of the night, when I'm walking through the darkness,
> You're my pillar of fire, to lead me on the way.
> Lord of the light, when the burning sun would scorch me,
> You're my Jonah's vine to shield me from the day.
> Lord of the body, when I cannot stand the hurting,
> You are healing of crippling and pain.
> Lord of the mind, when the Legion brings insanity,
> You're the word that restores me once again.[3]

KNOWING WHEN THINGS ARE BETTER

Like any other trauma, child sexual assault seems, at first, like it will never end. But with proper intervention, the initial symptoms will begin to disappear. The recovery process is never smooth. One child who wouldn't talk about her assault for months may suddenly begin to show signs of anger and fear about the time everything else seems to be returning to normal. A child may seem better and then start having nightmares again. This is to be expected. Setbacks are frustrating, but if the conditions are positive, a setback is, indeed, just part of the pathway to recovery.

Progress toward recovery is indicated by a decrease in the frequency and intensity of the symptoms previously identified. The child who was anxious and fearful will become less so as she recovers. The child who became withdrawn will begin to become more sociable and outgoing. A child is probably on the way to recovery when her grades improve, when she is able to play comfortably with her peers, and when she shows a willingness to take risks and try new things.

There may be a time after the crisis is past when the child wishes not to be reminded of the molestation in any way. She may have seemed to have forgotten about everything. This is a sign that a stage of reorganization and recovery is still ahead. With these stages there is likely to be a return of symptoms such as nightmares, bed-wetting, concentration problems, fears, and mood changes. This is normal. Continue to give support and encouragement. It is a phase that will usually pass.

As a child recovers, you may see her be able to set better boundaries for herself. She may not act in such sexual or seductive ways, and she will learn to meet needs for physical and emotional contact in a more appropriate manner. She can identify good and bad touches as well as other problematic behavior. She can verbalize her own lack of guilt and know the fault lies with the offender. Even the expression of anger and the knowledge of how it can be used are good bench marks of growth.

OBTAINING COUNSELING FOR YOUR CHILD

If, after a child has been sexually abused, she won't talk, seems to be holding something back, or has not returned to normal behavior even though several months have gone by, professional counseling is suggested. If the child was assaulted by a family member, *counseling is almost always needed.* Molested children will try to protect their parents from pain. They may not talk about their abuse because they don't think their parents can handle it. Incestual abuse devastates the entire family and requires intervention for *all* family members at some time or another.

David Peters in his excellent book, *A Betrayal of Innocence,* describes a number of factors that contribute to the total impact of abuse on a particular victim. While no list is all-inclusive, this material seems to summarize the damage factors quite well.

1. *The relationship of the molester to the victim:* The more closely related or highly trusted the molester, the more damage done to the child.
2. *The use of force or violence:* The more force or violence, the greater the damage, especially if serious physical injuries result.
3. *The degree of nonviolent coercion:* The greater the amount of fear and guilt used in controlling the victim, the more serious the damage.
4. *The extent of abuse:* Intercourse is more emotionally harmful than genital exposure or other noncontact forms of abuse. However, extensive and long-term fondling has been found in some instances to rival the damage caused by intercourse.
5. *The duration of abuse:* Sexual abuse which takes place over a long period of time tends to be more harmful than that of short duration.
6. *The number and frequency of incidents:* The more numerous and frequent the incidents, the greater the emotional damage.
7. *The age and developmental status of the victim:* Generally, the older the victim and the more aware she is of the nature of what occurred, the more serious the emotional harm done.
8. *The reactions of significant adults to the report of abuse:* The less emotional support the victim receives from her family members and the community, the greater the degree of damage.[4]

While there are always individual considerations, a general rule of thumb would be that where a child is subjected to a high level of harm in any one of these categories, counseling is strongly advised.

Almost all families who have experienced incestual child sexual abuse will need professional help. The total family system has been thrown into shock. The entire emotional climate is upset as spouses and children struggle with divergent loyalties and confused feelings of love, anger, shame, and guilt. It is questionable whether the family unit can stay together. Certainly things can no longer remain the way they were. Unfortunately, it is usually the victim who suffers most when a family chooses not to seek professional intervention.

Your first option is to seek a Christian counselor who is experienced and trained to work with children and child sexual abuse. Check out the counselor's qualifications by asking about his or her experience in working with abused children and families. Have the counselor describe his or her general approach to treatment. While not a hard and fast rule, evidence suggests that individual therapy, supplemented by group therapy, is most appropriate for children abused outside of their family by a nontrusted stranger.

In contrast, most of the current incest treatment programs use group counseling as the primary form of intervention, supplemented by specialized individual therapy as needed. Often separate groups are available for victims, offenders, non-offending spouses and/or family members, and adults who were abused as children.

The counselor should be sensitive to the needs of abused children. Establishing a good relationship with a child requires the counselor to be able to convey interest, warmth, sincerity, and respect. Also ask about the kind of training the counselor has received. Without specialized training (most of it obtained after graduate school), the counselor is not properly equipped to deal with the complex problems found in abused children and their families.

If you can't find a Christian counselor, you may be reluctant to work with a non-Christian counselor or agency. The reality is there are not enough trained Christian counselors to meet the demand. But it is also true that a well-trained and ethical counselor will not seek to undermine your or the child's Christian beliefs or values. Talk to people who have worked with the counselor and try to determine his or her success ratio. If families have been helped, and the cries of children comforted and restored, then actively seek such a counselor's assistance.

Check on the availability of victim compensation funds in your state to help with the cost of treatment. While originally designed for victims of physical assault or families of homicide victims, some states are adding benefits for domestic violence. These funds, while limited, can be used for medical and counseling expenses. Check with your local police department, State Office of the Attorney General, or departments of Labor or Industries for more information and application procedures. You may also have recourse through the courts to order the offender to pay for counseling costs separate from any state compensation.

GOALS OF COUNSELING

The first priority of most treatment programs is to help the victim deal with her feelings of blame, guilt, anger, and ambivalence toward herself, the offender, and the rest of her family. Victims who have experienced severe physical and emotional trauma will probably be candidates for therapy lasting up to two years or more. The smaller the base of support, the longer it will take for a child to regain her emotional strength. If the family is not making progress as a whole, the child will also be slower to recover.

If the offender is a parent or parent-figure who lives with the victim, it will take longer to overcome the problems of trust, security, role confusion, and so forth. Some particularly important areas of adjustment for victims are summarized in the following pages, as adapted from my book for counselors and pastors, *Counseling for Family Violence and Abuse*.[5]

Repressed anger and hostility. Though they may appear passive and compliant, most child sexual abuse victims are inwardly seething with anger and hostility. They are angry at the one who exploited them. They are also angry with parents or family members who did not protect them. Their anger may be expressed in depression or withdrawal as well as in physical complaints and aggressive fantasies, stories, drawings, or behavior.

Counseling should help the victim get in touch with her repressed feelings and learn to express anger in healthy, nondestructive ways. She should be encouraged to be assertive in her expression. Her feelings need to be supported, and the basic message given that it is OK to feel angry. The goal is to learn how to handle it well.

As a parent, be ready to accept some awkward attempts by your child to express her angry feelings. Be prepared for some surprising verbal outbursts. Your child will suddenly stand up for her rights on issues or circumstances that had previously been ignored. Don't criticize her feelings, but help redirect the form the anger has taken.

Inability to trust. A child who has been victimized by a trusted person will have difficulty in trusting anyone else in the future. The depth of her distrust will depend on how traumatic the consequences were of the shattered promises and betrayal.

A child will develop trust slowly and only with positive experiences. Satisfying relationships are the best medicine to help overcome the child's feelings of alienation. Help your child by encouraging her to try new relationships that have a good chance of success. Ask the school to match your child up with a particularly loving and consistent teacher. Put the bug in the ear of a trustworthy coach or scout leader so they can redouble their efforts to involve your child in healthy activities.

Blurred role boundaries and role confusion. Victims have experienced role confusion due to the trespassed boundaries between themselves and the offender. If an adult in a power position takes advantage of a less powerful child for a sexual relationship, a crossing of the usual societal role boundaries occurs. Though the sexual activity for the adult is primarily in the service of nonsexual needs, the sexual experience for the child generates a great deal of confusion. The confusion is magnified when the perpetrator is a family member.

The victim needs help to resolve her role confusion despite her past experience. Other family members should support the child's attempts to set appropriate boundaries. This might include rules for entering bedrooms or bathrooms when someone else is present, borrowing clothes or toys, and assigning unique tasks and responsibilities.

If at all possible, the offender, at some point, should explain to the child how the boundaries were crossed. The offender should acknowledge that he or she was responsible for the abuse, that the sexual behavior was inappropriate and will not be repeated. This may be a good time to approach the topic of forgiveness between the offender and the victim. Some ideas about forgiveness are presented in more detail in chapter 8, and should be considered for their application in sharing with a victimized child.

Self-mastery and control. Sexual abuse involves a violation of the victim's body, privacy, and rights of self-mastery. The child has been forced by someone in a more powerful position to do something wrong and unhealthy. The right to make decisions about her own space or territory was violated by someone who was supposedly trustworthy.

The result is often a child who avoids decisions or resists the decisions of others. The effects can be long-lasting and very destructive.

Parents have a vital part in helping the child learn self-mastery and control over elements in her world. This involves accountability, responsible behavior toward others and oneself, and the freedom to make one's own choices.

Your child needs opportunities to test her capacity for decision-making. She needs the freedom to make mistakes and to learn from them. Good judgment is achieved through practice. Allow her to be responsible for her own actions, and provide feedback that is not harsh or punitive.

Recanting. In about 30 percent of the cases, a child will either deny sexual abuse ever took place, despite strong corroboration, or will later say her story was not true. In cases of incest, the following pressures on a child might cause her to falsely deny her abuse.

- [ ] Threats by the offender that something bad will happen unless the child changes her story.
- [ ] Guilt about upsetting the family, perhaps by the father's having to leave home.
- [ ] Worry about the mother falling apart and not being able to care for the child or rest of the family.
- [ ] Feelings of rejection and ostracism by the family.
- [ ] Infatuation with the offender. The victim may have very pleasant feelings toward the person involved. The abuse may have been the only source of nurturance for the child and she doesn't want to lose that source.

☐ Pleasurable feelings about the experience and perhaps wanting some aspect of the relationship to continue.

☐ Fear regarding the court proceedings. The stress of the testimony process is greater than the desire to convince others of the truth.

☐ The need for acceptance and security, perceived so crucial to her survival that it is not worth going through with her story. The non-offending parent must help with these security needs if the child is going to hold up during the long and troubling recovery process.[6]

GOALS FOR THE FAMILY

The second major priority of most treatment programs is the restoration of the family itself. At a certain point in the treatment process it is appropriate and necessary to bring the family into focus. The purpose of family therapy is to develop a functional and healthy family unit free of any incestuous bond. The primary goals for the treatment of the incestuous family are: (1) for the child and mother to regain a sense of control over their own lives; (2) for the mother and father to become conscious of and to assume the expected parental roles, especially toward the victimized child; (3) for the mother and father to resume a mature marital relationship where their sexual needs are mutually satisfied; and (4) for all family members to resume interdependent roles without the incestuous elements.

Treatment of the family is aimed at helping each person move out of his or her isolated, trapped, hopeless, patterns of living into a greater sense of freedom and ability to make sound choices. The following general objectives provide an idea of where the treatment process is headed. Adjustments will always be necessary for the unique needs of your family.[7]

1. To increase each family member's belief in his or her ability to change from counterproductive patterns to more effective ways of behaving.
2. To learn how to balance the needs of the abused child with the needs of the family.
3. To help parents learn that their spouses cannot meet all of their emotional needs.

4. To encourage the parents and child to use people or activities as sources of support. Parents must learn how to turn to others for support when they feel overwhelmed or in need of specific help.
5. To assist the family in improving their interactional patterns within and outside of the family.
6. To help the family improve their self-esteem.
7. To encourage the family to decrease their social and emotional isolation, and to increase their interest in pursuing friendships, extended family relationships, church involvements, or activities outside of the home.
8. To improve the family's communication skills so they will be more in touch with their feelings and better able to communicate in an open and direct fashion.
9. To help the family make their emotional rules more explicit so they can be more flexible and responsive to the needs and protection of each member.
10. To work with the husband and wife to improve their relationship in order to lessen their fear of rejection or loss of one another.
11. To help the incest offender take full responsibility for the behavior and be able to verbalize this responsibility to the abused child and to the other family members.
12. Where appropriate, to help the offender's spouse take full responsibility for being an ineffective parent and enable her to refrain from projecting responsibility and blame onto the abused child or other people.
13. To inform the victim who to contact and what to do should molestation occur again.
14. To help family members learn to respect privacy and individuality within the family.
15. To redistribute power within the family so that one parent is not in dictatorial control of the rest of the family.
16. To teach the need for distinctions between generations. Adults need to act as adults. Children need to be seen and able to act as children.
17. To clarify family roles.
18. To help spouses find mutual emotional and sexual satisfaction together.

19. To help family members learn to distinguish fantasy from reality.
20. To teach parents to provide sexual education and protection for the child.
21. To enable parents to openly discuss their own upbringing and to recognize how they allowed sexual molestation to occur within their family.
22. As Christians, to explore the concepts of confession, forgiveness, grace, and growth through pain and suffering. The family needs to know growth does not always come by eliminating all of life's problems but by learning how to apply God's principles to the problems.

These goals and objectives only touch on the major themes of need for victims and their families. There is enough here, however, to enable you to ask appropriate questions and gauge progress as you seek help.

Remember God is the Great Physician. He Himself says, "I will restore you to health and heal your wounds" (Jeremiah 30:17).

Participation in the counseling process is important, but seeking the healing touch of Christ is most crucial of all. The treatment and prevention of child sexual abuse makes an important distinction between good and bad touches. It was the bad touches that led to the devastation and trauma. As Christians, we have the promise of the Christ who brought healing to those He touched (Luke 22:51). We see the *cleansing* touch of Christ when He cured the leper (Matthew 8:3); the *quieting* touch of Christ when He lifted the fever of Peter's mother-in-law (Matthew 8:15); the *illuminating* touch of Jesus when He opened the eyes of the blind men (Matthew 9:29); and the *reassuring* touch of Jesus to those who were afraid (Matthew 17:7). And finally, we see Christ giving a special touch to *children* (Mark 10:13, 16).

My heart goes out to those who have experienced the evil effects of abuse. But with the concluding lines of the classic poem by Myra Brooks Welch, I claim for you the healing *Touch of the Master's Hand.*

He's going and almost gone.
But the Master comes, and the foolish crowd
Can never quite understand, the worth of a soul

81

And the change that's wrought
By the touch of the Master's hand.

NOTES

1. Portions of this section include material adapted from Carolyn M. Byerly, *The Mother's Book: How to Survive the Incest of Your Child* (Dubuque, Iowa: Kendall/Hunt), 1985, pp. 11-13.
2. J.R. Conte and Lucy Berliner, "Sexual Abuse of Children: Implications for Practice," *Social Casework*, vol. 62, 1981, pp. 601-606.
3. *Lord of the Troubled Sea.* Words and music by Ken and Jane Medema. Copyright 1977, Word. All rights reserved. Used by permission.
4. David B. Peters, *A Betrayal of Innocence* (Waco, Texas: Word), 1986, p. 120.
5. Grant L. Martin, *Counseling for Family Violence and Abuse,* (Waco, Texas: Word), 1987.
6. Ibid., p. 198.
7. Ibid., pp. 233-234.

CHAPTER SIX

Preventing Further Tears

Reducing the Risk of Child Sexual Abuse

Caren's grandfather began molesting her when she was three. Caren later told a counselor how her grandfather's touches and the "way he had me sit on his lap" was different from anything she had experienced earlier. "It didn't feel right," she said. "My mom and dad were even in the room and I looked at them to come get me." But her parents did not recognize her unspoken plea for help.

Thinking no one cared about what was happening, Caren didn't tell anyone about her grandfather's actions. As a result, the abuse continued until she was twelve and finally had the courage to speak up. Even at the age of three, Caren felt something was wrong. She knew she didn't like it, but she lacked the ability to make the abuse stop and to get help.

Children often can sense that something is wrong before abuse actually occurs. There is a significant difference between affection and abuse. When touching crosses the line from one to another, children understand the difference. If we will teach our children to listen to this inner voice—this natural alarm system—and to speak up, we will have done much to prevent child sexual abuse. We don't need to discourage children from being naturally affectionate. But we do need to teach them to tell us if they experience something they don't like. Then we need to be ready to listen to and believe them when they tell us.

Therefore, the first line of defense in preventing sexual abuse is to ensure open communication between you and your child. One of the basic functions of communication is that it allows us to tell others how we feel and what we need. The other side of the coin is listening to and understanding the expressions of others so we can respond to their needs in a meaningful way.

As parents, we want to teach our children how to express their needs and feelings. Three channels must be navigated to accomplish this goal. All three are important. First, we must *model* positive communication to our children as we relate to the rest of our family. Our example before our children must demonstrate effective skills in sending and receiving messages of feelings and expectations. If a child sees his parents give each other the silent treatment for three days after a disagreement, that child is more likely to avoid expressing his own feelings in a time of crisis because "that's what Mom and Dad do when they are sad."

Second, parents need to provide *instruction* in communication. This includes specific directions for your child on recognizing his own feelings, realizing feelings are OK to have, and expressing those feelings in clear and direct ways. This can be done using children's books or recordings about feelings, through discussions around the dinner table, or by telling stories to your child.

I remember as a young child sitting in my grandfather's lap and listening to fascinating tales about animal characters such as Charlie the Chipmunk. Drawn from his experiences as an educator, naturalist, and farmer, "Papa" always included a moral to his impromptu creations about beavers, chipmunks, rabbits, and bears. His creatures had feelings which reflected his own empathetic nature, and I'm sure some of my values were influenced by his instruction in fables and metaphor.

Third, the ability to communicate will be influenced by the kind of *consequences* parents provide to the child's attempts to express herself. For example, if a child comes into the family room while Dad is reading the paper and asks, "Why do people get mad?" only to be ignored, that child is less likely to ask questions or volunteer information on future occasions. Encouraging meaningful communication consists of taking the time to listen to fractured ramblings about your child's latest fantasy friend, as well as the more serious revelations.

A nine-year-old girl told the authorities her uncle had been molesting her for a long time. When asked why she hadn't told her parents, the girl said, "I tried to tell my mom once, but she didn't listen. She was too busy."

It's easy for parents to get so caught up in their own problems that the child feels Mom and Dad are too busy to care. Make sure you take the time to listen, and don't disregard or dismiss your child's statements. If your child learns you can be counted on to listen to his make-believe stories, he will more likely trust you with a secret about abuse that somebody told him not to tell.

PREVENTING HIGH-RISK BEHAVIOR IN CHILDREN

Chapter 2 identified several characteristics of children which make them a higher risk for abuse. Those who sexually abuse children seek out victims who are easily controlled or manipulated. A more assertive child will be seen by a potential abuser as one who will say no, fight back, or refuse to keep the secret. There is no way parents can supervise their child all the time. Thus the first means of prevention is the child herself. We must teach our children the difference between being obedient and remaining bold if power and authority is being misused.

Christian parents teach their children to "respect your elders" and to "obey those in authority." These same teachings can make our children more vulnerable to abuse. Teach your child about the misuse of authority. Obedience is important, but also emphasize the importance of moral courage such as found in Daniel, Esther, and Peter. Instruct your child to take strong action when any adult suggests she do something wrong. Tell her it is OK to scream or run away if the adult does not stop.

We also do our children a disservice when we tell them never to be a tattletale. Explain to them that tattling is telling on someone the same age or on a brother or sister so you can get them into trouble. If your child has a problem, a friend needs help, or an older person is bothering him, it is *not* tattling. We should tell our children, "If an adult tells you not to tell anyone else about what he is doing, you should tell—because it is probably something wrong." The following examples will help make the distinction clear.

> Would it be tattling if Jimmy's big brother was hurting him all the time and you told me about it? It would not, because Jimmy needs someone to help him.

> * * * * *

> If you saw a classmate steal a candy bar from the corner grocery store, would it be tattling to tell me about it? No, because that classmate has done something wrong that needs correction.

> * * * * *

> If your teacher or coach asked you to look at some pictures or touched you and asked you not to tell, would it be tattling when you told me? It would not, because someone older is trying to get you to do something that is wrong.

You may also want to establish a *No More Secrets* rule in your family. This is an agreement that no one in the family will keep secrets, and if asked to keep a secret, the child can respond with, "No, we don't keep secrets in our family and I'm going to tell." Surprises are fine. A surprise is something that makes people happy and will be disclosed eventually. A secret, on the other hand, is never supposed to be told. Even a four-year-old can agree not to talk about Dad's birthday present because it is a surprise, not a secret. One of the things an offender looks for is a child who will keep secrets. If the child refuses, it's likely the offender will consider her too risky a chance. We don't want our children victimized because of a wrongly placed code of honor that says, "I promised him I wouldn't tell."

One large class of risk factors is anything that makes a child feel emotionally insecure, needy, or unsupported. A child who feels insecure will be more vulnerable to the seduction or grooming behavior of a potential abuser. When the abuser offers attention, affection, or bribes, an insecure or unsupported child will have no one else to turn to, or will be more afraid to tell.

This means parents need to do all they can to meet the emotional needs of their children within the home. Many books have been written on this topic by such authors as Dr. James Dobson in his books *Dare to Discipline, Hide or Seek,* and *The Strong-Willed Child.* Space does not allow a detailed presentation on how to improve a child's self-esteem. So only a few summary comments will be made.

There are four components to building self-esteem and confidence in a child: a sense of security, a sense of belonging, a sense of competency, and a sense of purpose.

1. *Sense of security.* The first component of a realistic appraisal of oneself is to have experience in a family where there is order, structure, and predictability. The goal in building a child's sense of security is to set realistic limits for her behavior, followed by consistent enforcement of the rules. If the child is allowed to talk back to her mother one day, but disciplined the next, two things will happen. First, the behavior is more likely to happen again, because the nature of most children is to see how far they can push their parents' inconsistency. Second, the child is going to be more insecure. Children need and inwardly desire protective limitations.

Imagine trying to drive across a two-lane bridge built high over a deep chasm, below which is a raging river full of hungry crocodiles. The problem is that this particular bridge has absolutely no sides or guardrails. The pavement simply drops off for hundreds of feet to the river below. Think of how you would feel as you were driving across such a bridge. Most people would drive with hesitancy, moving slowly ahead and perhaps in an unsteady manner. Perhaps they would drive down the middle of the road, taking other people's share of the highway for safety's sake. Some might even drive as fast as possible to get the anxiety over with as quickly as possible.

A child may act in one of these ways when no guidelines or loving structure exist to give her confidence and a sense of security. A child desires an appropriate amount of control, but insists her parents earn the right to manage that control. Scripture suggests our love is shown in the way we discipline our children and if that system of order is absent, our love is also absent (Proverbs 3:11-12; 13:24).

A final word on security is the importance of building trust.

Parents must keep their word. If you make promises to a child, those promises should be kept, even when it is difficult (Psalm 15:4). This applies to possible restrictions or punishments if a child breaks a rule as well as rewards for good behavior. Circumstances beyond your control will sometimes arise. Disappointments are part of living, but a parent's word should be kept at all reasonable costs.

2. *Sense of belonging.* A child needs to feel he is a part of something bigger than himself. His foundational membership is in the family. Your child should be proud to belong to your family—not that your family is necessarily better than anybody else's, just that he knows yours is unique, special, and rewarding.

There are many ways to encourage this sense of closeness and community. Budget time for family events; establish family routine and traditions; plan activities that foster fun and unity. For example, it is an un-American violation of the highest degree if our family doesn't have clam chowder and play board games on Christmas Eve. This started when I was a child and was just one of those little things that made our family unique.

Engage in things that build family identity and pride. One year our church had each family make a felt banner to be hung in the sanctuary during the Christmas season. Though standardized by size, each family used its own creativity and talent to prepare patterns, figures, and graphics that captured its own distinctive themes, interests, and values. The project was not only fun, but it helped bond those special elements that were part of our family.

A sense of belonging also has responsibilities. Chores and tasks go along with living together. While certainly not always greeted with enthusiasm, those daily demands are part of the cost of belonging and make membership more meaningful.

Avoid ridicule and excessive teasing. Jokes, humor, and surprises are certainly appropriate. This last Fourth of July, my oldest boy, Bryce, had to be at his job early in the morning. So about 5 A.M. I got up and wired an "auto bomb" to his newly acquired car. A bit later, when he turned on the ignition of his prized old Mustang, a cloud of blue smoke poured out from under the hood, a long whistle shrieked through the haze, after which reverberated a loud bang! Uncertain of whether World War III had started or merely a bad dream, Bryce turned to see Dad duck behind the bedroom curtain and realized the incident was not fatal.

Practical jokes and verbal sparring can help create a sense of community, but do not allow such antics to attack a person's character or demean his behavior.

Family is not the only group to which a child needs to belong. It is the base of operations, but she will join others such as Scouts, church youth groups, sports teams, musical groups, special interest clubs, and friendship groups. Encourage your child to become a member of other worthwhile groups. It is important to the development of her self-esteem.

3. *Sense of competency.* The third component of self-esteem is having a realistic value of what a child can do. This is the sweet smell of success. A child must learn to recognize and have good feelings about some of his abilities, interests, and values. A careful balance is needed, because society places a premium on physical beauty, material possession, and intelligence. Every child needs a "claim to fame." To achieve this, parents need to give positive feedback and provide the encouragement to try new things and take risks. Parents can recognize potential in their child and help cultivate that potential without applying undo pressure.

Above all, show unconditional love. Regardless of your child's abilities, let her know you love her. Don't compare him to other children. Recognize your child for who she is, unique from any other. Don't let your own unfulfilled dreams become an inappropriate burden for your child. I have seen children endure hours and hours of ice-skating lessons, for example, along with early morning practice schedules, only because it was so important to their mothers.

Finally, help your child compensate for her weaknesses. A nonathletic child can be guided into art, music, or academics, or vice versa. Sometimes it takes many false starts to find something your child really enjoys and will stick with for a long period. Keep at it. Seek professional help if necessary. Every child needs to have some areas where she can find success.

4. *Sense of purpose.* The final component of self-esteem is spiritual in nature. At some point in one's life, everybody asks, "Why am I here?" The Christian has a road map for life; God *does* have a plan for us. A sense of purpose is the understanding of how that plan works for each individual.

What is this purpose? From the beginning, God has given man

the task of subduing and ruling over the earth as His representatives (Genesis 1:26; 9:2; Psalm 8:6). We are also called to worship and honor our Creator (Deuteronomy 26:10; Psalm 95:6). We are asked to be wise and good stewards over creation (Luke 19:13; Romans 14:12). As stewards of all that God created, we are to bear fruit (John 15:16).

We are encouraged to use our abilities and gifts in service for others (Matthew 3:8; Romans 7:4; Philippians 1:10-11). If obedient to this purpose, the fruits of love, joy, peace, patience, kindness, goodness, faithfulness, gentleness, and self-control will be nourished and multiplied (Galatians 5:22-23).

Specific decisions can be made and plans established in the context of this heavenly purpose. Certainly, the concept should not be ignored until time to choose a college or career. Wise parents should start early to instruct their children why we are here. Participation in Sunday School and church will contribute to a child's learning. But through example, instruction, and prayer, parents should make every effort to educate their children about where they are going and how to get there. The type of instruction will vary depending on the age of the child. Do not ignore it. Such a sense of direction and goals make a major contribution to self-esteem and self-confidence.

GIVE YOUR CHILD KNOWLEDGE

A child's ability to resist or avoid abuse may also be lowered because she is naive or lacks information. The following concepts seem particularly relevant to preventing child sexual abuse:

- [ ] God loves you just the way you are.
- [ ] You have a mind that can help you avoid danger.
- [ ] Your body belongs to you and is specially made.
- [ ] There are private parts of your body.
- [ ] There are many kinds of touches: some good, some bad.
- [ ] You have a right to say who touches you and how.
- [ ] If someone touches you in a way you don't like or in a way you think is wrong, it's OK to say no.
- [ ] If the person doesn't stop, say, "I'm going to tell," and then tell, no matter what they say or do.
- [ ] If you are asked to keep a secret, refuse.

☐ Someone older may threaten you by saying something bad will happen if you tell. This is wrong and you should tell somebody right away.

☐ Getting away is very important when you sense danger.

☐ If you have a problem, keep talking about it until someone believes and helps you.

Several books by Christian authors do a good job of covering most of these concepts. *Protecting Your Children from Sexual Assault* by William Katz is part of the "Little Ones Teaching Kit."[1] The kit includes the parents' teaching guide and an activity workbook. The material is Bible-oriented and intended to help the parent effectively communicate to children the reality of sexual assault. The workbook can be taught in approximately eight sessions of thirty to sixty minutes, and the content adapted to both primary and intermediate age children.

Child Abuse! What You Can Do About It[2] by Angela Carl is another useful resource, perhaps a bit more extensive than the Katz book. The activity workbook is titled, *Good Hugs and Bad Hugs: How Can You Tell?* The material is adaptable to children in grades K-6 and has a definite Christian focus.

Another quality resource is Joy Berry's "Danger Zones" children series published by Word.[3] The three books—*Kidnapping, Abuse and Neglect,* and *Sexual Abuse*—are colorful, written to be read by children between the ages of six and twelve, and cover most of the concepts outlined earlier. The *Sexual Abuse* book does a good job of identifying the various ploys used by sexual abusers to get their victims to cooperate, but does not relate any of the concepts to biblical references.

Other resources are listed in a special section at the end of this book. Most are available at your local bookstore.

RULES ABOUT STRANGERS

While the majority of abusers are known to the child, we must not ignore the possibility of abuse by a stranger. The following list of recommendations will reduce the risk of sexual molestation by someone outside the child's family.

1. *Do not leave your child alone in one part of a store while*

you shop in another. Your child may fuss about wanting to stay in the toy department while you go buy a tube of toothpaste, but don't take the chance.

2. *Don't allow a young child to go into a public restroom alone.* If you can't go with her, remain outside, and tell her to yell if there is a problem.

3. *Be careful about leaving a child alone in the car while running errands.* While more convenient, it may not be worth the risk. At least lock the doors, take the keys, and instruct your child not to unlock the door for anyone. (Some localities consider it a crime to leave young children unattended in a car.)

4. *Be careful about letting young children play in unsecured areas.* If she's under five, keep your eye on your child at all times. Don't let your child wander.

5. *Always know where your older child is going.* As they get older, children need more freedom, but don't let them walk alone in questionable areas. Require they keep you informed of their destinations and time lines.

6. *Instruct your child on how to answer phone calls.* A child should never reveal she is home alone. A possible response is, "My mom can't come to the phone right now. Can she call you back in a little while?" Similar caution should be taught for answering the door. Question why you should ever leave young children home alone.

7. *Photograph your child regularly and have him or her fingerprinted.* Keep the photos and prints in a safe place in case you need them for an emergency.

8. *Emphasize to your child she is to contact you immediately when she is hurt or in trouble even if her problem resulted from breaking a rule.* Assure her you will come to her aid regardless of the circumstances. Teach young children how to make emergency phone calls.

9. *Teach and illustrate the following Rules about Strangers:*
   ☐ A stranger is anyone a child does not know.
   ☐ Children cannot tell the good guys from the bad guys just by looking or talking to them.
   ☐ Children are the only ones able to keep themselves safe all of the time.
   ☐ Children should listen to their brain when it tells

them something is dangerous.
- [ ] Stay at least an arm's reach away from strangers.
- [ ] Don't talk to strangers, even if they know your name or something about you, unless you have agreed to use a code word.
- [ ] Don't take anything from strangers, not even something that belongs to you.
- [ ] Don't go anywhere with a stranger.[4]

CHOOSING CARETAKERS

As more and more mothers are working outside the home, a tremendous increase in the demand for child care has resulted. While the majority of child-care workers are dedicated persons, there is still an element of risk. Stories accumulate from all parts of the country involving sexual abuse by someone paid to care for children. Some child abusers will go to great lengths to find positions that give them convenient access to children. Parents must be diligent in choosing caretakers for their children.

Following are questions or considerations that can be used in selecting different kinds of caretakers. No list is complete. The items listed here are in addition to practical concerns such as cost, location, and appropriateness of curriculum for your child. Trust your instincts. If something makes you feel uncomfortable about a particular program or person, go someplace else.

Day-Care Centers

Facility
- [ ] Is the facility licensed? If not, why not?
- [ ] What is the general atmosphere?
- [ ] Is it clean and orderly?
- [ ] Are there separate bathroom facilities for children and adults?
- [ ] What is the child/staff ratio? (It should be at least one adult for every six children, and one adult for every four infants, though legal ratios vary nationwide.)
- [ ] Is there a list of parents who can be contacted as references?
- [ ] Ask for professional references.
- [ ] Check with those references. What are the strengths

and weaknesses of the center? How were problems dealt with in the past?

Staff

☐ Are the staff members actively interested in the children's activities, and do they seem to enjoy being with the children?

☐ How much of the staff's interaction is corrective ("no," "stop that") versus instructive or complimentary?

☐ Does the staff seem patient with the children?

☐ What is the training and day-care experience of different members of the staff?

☐ Has there been any check for previous criminal records?

☐ How long has each staff person been there?

☐ Are there any adult or teenage males who work there? If so, who, and in what capacity?

☐ Who do they use for substitutes? What are their credentials and how often are they used?

☐ Are staff members related to one another? If so, how? How long have they worked together? Were previous references checked?

☐ Do you notice staff members indiscreetly complaining about any particular children or families?

☐ What kind of discipline measures are used?

☐ Are there any other adolescents or adults present whose purpose is not clear, even if they are relatives of staff members?

Activities

☐ Are the children involved in their activities? Are they enjoying themselves?

☐ Is there a balance between planned activities and free time?

☐ Do I and my child feel comfortable here?

☐ Do the children seem to relate well to the staff members, and do they seem to trust them?

☐ Are you welcome to drop in anytime? If not, why? This is important.

☐ Is the children's work displayed? Is it current?

☐ Is there enough space for play and rest?

☐ Do the children watch any TV? Are there limits to the

amount of TV the children can watch?
- [ ] Are there proper arrangements for medical emergencies?

Supervision
- [ ] How is the free time supervised?
- [ ] What is the adult/child ratio throughout the different times of the day?
- [ ] Is the director present? If not, who is in charge?
- [ ] Are the children ever left with just one staff member? If so, what happens in an emergency?
- [ ] How secure is the facility? Could someone come in and pick up a child unnoticed?
- [ ] Is the playground secure? Are there blind spots where children can't be seen?
- [ ] How are messages handled? Is this a secure system?[5]

Once you have chosen a facility, continue to monitor the program. Make occasional unannounced visits to the center. Take time to observe the interaction between your child and the staff. Offer to help on field trips. Don't be afraid to ask questions.

Talk to your child about his experiences at the center. Be alert for any changes in your child's behavior. Follow up on any curious events. There is no guarantee, but if you have adequately screened the facility and taught your child how to protect himself, a major degree of safety is assured.

Baby-sitters

As we walk out the door for the evening, how often have we instructed our children, "Do everything the baby-sitter says"? That message contradicts everything I have been saying is necessary to keep our children safe. Baby-sitters have extended access to our children for many hours. There is no better opportunity for abuse to occur. Even screening the sitter carefully does not totally eliminate risk.

When the baby-sitter comes to your house, go over the ground rules in the presence of your children. Cover things like what they can eat, if and when they can watch TV, when they are to go to bed, whether they need a bath and how that is to be handled, if they need help in getting ready for bed, and any other procedures. Discussing this in front of everybody lessens the risk of manipulation by either the baby-sitter or your child. Tell the baby-sitter not to deviate from your guidelines, and that you have instructed the children to tell you if there are any changes or even the proposal of changes. Tell the sitter your children do not keep secrets and they will tell you if any secrets are mentioned. Leave telephone numbers and instructions for emergencies. If your child is ever uneasy about staying with a particular sitter, try to find out why.

You may want to establish a code word with your child that can be used to signal when something is wrong without letting the sitter become aware of it. You might use the name of a special toy, the cat, or a book title. While away, you can call home to check on things. If, while talking with your child, she uses the code word, you will know to ask more questions, call a neighbor, or come home.

Finally, consider the statistics that reveal that while females do abuse children, the vast majority of sexual abuse is done by males. This automatically excludes some excellent, well-mannered young men and boys from baby-sitting, but it's up to you to consider the risks and make the appropriate decision. Remember, the best defense your child will have against sexual abuse is the preventive training you have given her, and your own ability to communicate with her about what she really feels and thinks. And above all, pray for her protection, and pray continually (1 Thessalonians 5:17).

NOTES

1. William Katz, *Protecting Your Children from Sexual Assault*, Little Ones Books, P.O. Box 725, Young America, Minnesota 55399. $11.50 for parents' guide and activity workbook.
2. Angela R. Carl, *Child Abuse! What You Can Do About It*, and *Good Hugs and Bad Hugs: How Can You Tell?* (Cincinnati: Standard Publishing), 1985.
3. Joy Berry, *Alerting Kids to the Danger Zones: Sexual Abuse* (Waco, Texas: Word), 1984.
4. Adapted from Sherryll Kerns Kraizer, *The Safe Child Book* (New York: Dell), 1985, p. 83.
5. Ibid., pp. 101-110.

PART 2

Adults Who Hurt

CHAPTER SEVEN

Pains of the Past

Understanding the Trauma of Adults Sexually Abused as Children

This was more than he could handle. So the counseling intern called in his supervisor for help. The intern had been counseling with Becky, a thirty-five-year-old mother of two who had been active in the church. Her marriage was on the rocks, and her life had been an emotional roller coaster for years.

As a routine part of the interview, the counselor asked some questions about Becky's childhood. She immediately became very agitated. Over the next few minutes she deteriorated from a normal adult conversation to a hysterical outpouring of moans, tears, and screams. When the supervisor entered the room, Becky was curled up in a fetal-like position under the counselor's desk. She screamed when anyone came near her. It took another hour to calm her down, but after much reasurance and comforting, Becky seemed to snap out of her fearful trance.

The supervisor wanted to hospitalize her, but Becky refused, saying she had to take care of her family and didn't have time to be "put away." The next day she seemed fine and had no signs of her break from reality of the previous morning.

This incident was but the beginning of a long and frustrating road to emotional stability for Becky. The highly emotional scene was to repeat itself many times before she was done. Memories from her childhood would inevitably throw her into fits of terror, rage, and panic. Sometimes Becky would recall a portion of an old experience, but never did the whole picture emerge at once. Outside the counseling room, Becky would have flashbacks, images, and dreams. Often there was a dark ominous force present in her sensations. Her frequent feelings of panic, coercion, pain, and fear led her to drink even though her father had died from alcoholism.

Becky's family and social life reflected these same themes. She was bright and capable in many areas, but had trouble in seeing things through to conclusion. Many projects were started, but few were finished. For example, a knitted blanket for a relative's birthday was still half done, because Becky couldn't stand the prospect of rejection.

Conflict seemed to fill her home. Becky and her children seemed close one day and at each other's throats the next. Becky looked to her husband for support and comfort. But he responded with passive resistance and financial irresponsibility. Her poor relationship with her husband only served to reinforce Becky's distrust of close relationships. She was attracted to friendships within her church only to find herself putting up walls and refusing to let people see beyond the plastic mask she usually wore. Becky loved her mother, but at the same time could never feel comfortable around her.

The total picture of her abuse never really took shape. Becky and her counselor were sure she had been sexually abused as a child. The specific instances were never identified, along with continuing ambiguity about the person or persons who may have abused her. Each attempt to recall the details produced such catastrophic emotional reactions, Becky eventually told the counselor she could no longer pursue that course of inquiry. The counselor respected her wishes and worked with the details that were available.

Becky survived. There is no happy-ever-after ending to her story. As one who was probably abused as a child, she suffers scars even today. Her marriage did end in divorce, but Becky found the strength to go back to college, deal with the problems of her teenage children, and overcome some severe financial setbacks. Her story illustrates many of the issues to be discussed in this chapter. There is every reason to have hope. God wants His children to be whole and healthy. But just as Christians die in car accidents or undergo surgery for cancer, the trauma of childhood abuse can leave fatal or permanent scars. The effects of child sexual abuse make life more difficult in some areas. But victims of childhood abuse can make successful adjustments despite the hardships.

One of the first steps in the process is to realize that some of the problems in your life could be the result of having been sexually abused as a child. This chapter describes the typical symptoms and features of an adult victimized as a child. The next chapter will discuss how to deal with each of the major symptom areas on the road toward recovery and health.

SYMPTOMS IN ADULTS ABUSED AS CHILDREN

Following are some questions to ask yourself if you think you may have been abused as a child:

- ☐ Do you feel bad, inadequate, or inferior?
- ☐ Does life seem out of control? Do you feel powerless to change the course of events around you?
- ☐ Is it difficult to make and maintain friendships or intimate relationships?
- ☐ Do people seem to take advantage of you and use you for their purposes? Do you find yourself feeling resentful for letting it go on so long?
- ☐ Are you often giving and kind to other people, but find they often do not give much to you?
- ☐ Are you generally afraid and distrustful of others?
- ☐ Do you find yourself feeling bitter, suspicious, and angry much of the time?
- ☐ Do you have a hard time accepting compliments and favors from friends and family?

☐ Is life confusing, without much purpose or direction?

☐ Are you reluctant to socialize or meet new people?

☐ Do you have a poor relationship with your parent(s)? Have you tried to gain their acceptance without success? Have you been unable to talk about any but superficial things with either parent?

☐ Has self-control been a problem? Have you had problems with food, alcohol, drugs, money, or sex?

☐ Have there been times when you have been abusive to your children, or have worried that you might be an unfit parent?

Many people can answer yes to *some* of these questions *once in a while,* but adults who have been abused as children tend to have positive responses to *many* of these questions *on a regular basis.* Their struggles will have lasted most of their lives, and often have been intense. Childhood abuse is difficult to admit. Because you were never hospitalized, exposed to the legal process, or it only happened once does not mean no negative effects resulted. All types of abuse—physical, emotional, or sexual—can leave their marks on children. The first step is to make the connection between that early experience and the current symptoms.

Denial. All of us tend to forget strong, unpleasant events. This lack of recall protects us from the pain often associated with traumatic memories. Denial keeps us safe from that pain. It is also the first stage in the process of grief or loss. Therefore, if one is stuck on denial, it means he has never finished the process of dealing with his loss.

Becky had a difficult time moving past her denial. Some aspects of her abuse were apparently so traumatic she could never identify all the specifics. Not knowing the source of her abuse made it difficult to work through the dynamics of anger and bitterness. She knew someone had probably violated her trust, but who? Some kind of event had left a lifetime of scars on her emotions. She felt rage toward that person. But movement away from that resentment was difficult because she couldn't know for sure who was responsible for her pain.

Becky was an exception, however. Most victims of abuse can eventually recall enough of the elements of their trauma to adequately deal with their loss.

Confusion. During the abuse, and for years after it has stopped, the victim can be very confused. Something has happened that neither the child nor adult victim can understand. How was she supposed to respond to the abuse? If she has kept the secret all these years, chances are she was never taught to say no or that it was OK to tell. Boundaries were crossed. Someone with power and a position of trust exploited the child by making her a sexual partner. The child then wonders about the appropriate use of power and authority. That same question continues into adulthood. If married, the adult victim remains confused about love and sex, obedience and control. She also has problems with trust and fear, as well as believing in God's protection. If this confusion continues, the victim is vulnerable to excessive feelings of anger, fear, shame, and guilt. Without knowing what is normal, many adult victims are frightened even more. Let's look at each of these feelings.

FEELINGS EXPERIENCED BY ADULT VICTIMS

Anger. The victim is angry at the abuser for what he has done. The victim may also be angry at herself for participating in the abuse. The victim might even be angry at the non-offending members of her family for not preventing the abuse or for how the family handled the disclosure, if indeed disclosure ever occurred. Often the female victim of incest remains angry at her mother for not protecting her.

You may feel that you have been violated, betrayed, exploited, and unjustly treated. The question may often arise, "Why me?" If the awareness of abuse comes to light as an adult, you may find that the love and fondness for your parents may disapper, replaced by hate.

The anger experienced by most victims is usually either *bitterness*—the provoked, exasperated anger that nurses a long-standing grudge (Ephesians 6:4), or *resentment*—the suppressed, enduring desire to retaliate or seek revenge (Ephesians 4:31; Colossians 3:8). Both of these forms of anger, while understandable, can eat away at your soul and spirit.

Other victims have to deal with anger toward themselves. They are fearful of what will happen if they express their true feelings. The anger may be so strong they are afraid they might do something violent. They may then overcontrol themselves, even to the point of acting compulsive.

Fear. There is much for the victim of child sexual abuse to fear. As a child, there is the fear of physical pain and damage. There is the implied threat by the offender. There is the fear of not being believed if you tell or of the consequences to the offender and the rest of the family should the secret come to light. These, as well as the fear of blame, punishment, having to talk to strangers, appear in court, or having the abuse occur again, often cause the child to feel fearful all the time. This generalized fear can continue throughout the victim's lifetime, making worry and anxiety a constant companion. As an adult, you might not be able to identify the source of the fear. You just know your stomach is tied up in knots much of the time, and you seldom feel safe and secure.

Shame. The victim of abuse may feel dirty, embarrassed, and ashamed. You may feel you are the only person this ever happened to, or that you are different from anyone else. You may fear rejection if other people were to find out. Many clients have told me they were fearful of telling their husbands about their abuse because of potential negative reactions. Victims often feel defective, like damaged goods, soiled for life. Others are embarrassed by the knowledge they have come from a disturbed family where the father used a child for the satisfaction of sexual desires.

Guilt. The child and adult victims of sexual abuse often feel guilty for what has happened. You may believe the abuse was all your fault. If the abuse was ever pleasurable or if you received special privileges from the offender, the feelings of guilt may be even more pronounced.

Victims sometimes feel guilty because they didn't try harder to stop the abuse, or because they didn't tell sooner. You may feel guilty for having any fond feelings for the abuser, or for being angry at other family members for not protecting you. If the abuse was reported, you may feel guilty for seeing the abuser put in prison, or for the family being disrupted by the proceedings. The situation can be made even worse if the family blames you in any way.

Low self-esteem. The victim of sexual abuse has been treated as an object rather than a person. Because of the abuse, she may feel ugly, bad, helpless, and worthless. In the eyes of a child, to be hurt intentionally by an adult means she was bad. Most children will place the badness within themselves rather than in their parents, whom they desire to love. Abused children tend to make rigid divisions in the way they think. Things are either good or bad. If the victim sees herself as all bad, she will view her parents, including the incest offender, as all good. The tendency is for the victim to grow up viewing herself as bad and everybody else as good, or at least better.

Adults abused as children tend to think, "If my own parents thought I was no good, how can anybody love me?" That sets up a self-fulfilling prophecy. Because victims don't expect much from others, they make very few requests. Victims often cannot identify and express their own needs. Since they don't state their needs very well, other people don't do a very good job of meeting any of the victims' legitimate needs. This reinforces the victims' opinion that they don't deserve any good things because they are so bad.

Victims also tend to believe that no one could ever love them if they knew the truth. This low self-esteem leads some victims to be further victimized throughout their life. Women who were abused often choose husbands who are more likely to be abusive to their wives—and children. Victims of sexual abuse, particularly men, have a higher chance of becoming sexual abusers themselves.

A low self-image can also lead to continual depression and thoughts of suicide. Some victims show problems in self-control and act out their emotions in antisocial ways such as delinquency, shoplifting, sexual promiscuity, or prostitution. Sometimes a female incest victim will tend to relate to men in primarily sexual ways, perpetuating her dilemma. As a teenager or adult, the victim of incest may feel out of place with others her own age because she lacks good social skills. Victims tend to act older than they really are, but feel quite insecure.

Lack of trust. Trust is a major issue for adults abused as children. They have trouble trusting their own thoughts, feelings, and reactions as well as the intentions of others. Because most abusers held a position of trust with the victim, the ability to relate to trustworthy people was damaged very early. Since this trust was broken, it is very difficult to restore. Many victims

105

experience a vicious cycle. The less they trust, the less likely they are to have close friends and intimate relationships. They don't take many social or emotional risks. Without the reinforcement of satisfying friendships, these women become more isolated and believe more strongly they cannot trust others. The absence of social success drives them further into retreat and isolation. Consequently, they never learn how to be open and trusting in an appropriate manner.

Some victims may have difficulties with people of the same sex or with physical characteristics similar to the abuser. Many victims experience problems in sexual adjustment in marriage because of their inability to relax and trust their partner. These victims, as children, may have developed the idea that sex was evil and shameful and never outgrew this belief. To cope with their abuse, some victims learned to turn off their body sensations. They may have gone into a trance or stared at the ceiling to protect themselves from the pain and anguish of the abuse. Now they may have trouble eliminating that old survival habit, even though they want to enjoy sex with their spouse.

UNDERSTANDING THE SOURCE OF YOUR PAIN

You were not responsible for the sexual abuse that may have happened to you as a child. You *are* responsible for choosing how you think, feel, and act *now*. With God's help, you must decide how you will live the rest of your life. God has made available specific tools for your understanding and growth. I cannot promise you total relief from every symptom mentioned earlier. The scars of sexual abuse, whether occurring as a child or adult, can be devastating. But you can be free from denial and overwhelming feelings of bitterness, resentment, terror, guilt, and fear. I will first discuss how to get in touch with the specific details of the abuse. In the next chapter, I will go back over the symptoms most commonly found in adult victims of abuse and point out some ways to deal with the specific feelings and experiences.

Breaking through denial. Before any other remedies can be applied, you must bring to consciousness the specific details, pictures, and feelings of the abuse. Even if you have pushed much of the memory into your unconscious, it is important to be able to remember what you saw, heard, felt, and understood as a victim.

This can be a very painful experience and you may need the help of an experienced counselor. But such information will help reduce some of the confusion you may feel about the experience. It also allows God to deal with each and every aspect of the abuse. It is much like cancer surgery. Very often the question asked of the surgeon is, "Did you get all of it?"

Begin by calling on the Holy Spirit to help bring to mind the parts of your experience needing recollection. Unplug the phone, turn off the radio, choose a time when you won't be interrupted, and spend time in prayer and reflection. Don't expect everything to come to you at once. Memories may come in fragments, partial impressions, pictures, and fleeting ideas. It is a good idea to keep a pencil and paper close by to record your impressions. You might even try using a tape recorder to free you from the mechanics of writing.

If you have some knowledge of your abuse, you can go back to the specific time and place rather quickly. If that is true, try to recall all of the relevant parts—who, when, where, and what. What were your feelings, thoughts, and reactions to each aspect of the events? Tears and anguish are not uncommon in sessions like this, and that is another reason why it is best to have the help of a trusted friend or counselor during the process. The goal is to identify any event that has pain attached to it. Enter the various events and your reactions in your diary or journal.

If you have no idea of the specifics of your abuse, the process may take longer. You might try to reconstruct your childhood from the earliest age you can remember. Going back through family photograph albums may help activate forgotten events and people. Memory often comes back in bits and pieces, so there is nothing too insignificant to record.

Read books or listen to tapes about abuse, incest, or the healing of memories. David Seamands' book, *Healing of Memories,* or Norman Wright's *Making Peace with Your Past* are good resources.[1]

Reviewing high school- and college yearbooks or annuals may bring some associations to mind. Taking a trip back to the family home or community where the abuse might have occurred may also be helpful. Hometowns, churches, schools, play fields, or other landmarks might be used by God to bring back important feelings.

Talk to family members. A client of mine was having difficulty reconciling how her family had dealt with her abuse. With much reluctance she talked with her grandmother and found out a great deal of important information. It also broke lose a barrier between her and the grandmother she had never understood. This also made the grandmother's death, a short time later, much easier to handle.

The family secret may have been kept for years. So your search may require judicious inquiry. Don't let continued fear keep you from acquiring the knowledge you need to help regain your emotional health.

Your goal is to develop a list, in approximate chronological order, of all components of your victimization. It should be as specific as possible to allow you to deal with each person, event, and feeling associated with that event.

If you can't make progress by yourself, obtain the help of a professional counselor experienced in dealing with adults victimized as children.

Here is a poem written by a client who struggled for a long time with her abusive past. After much effort she was able to put aside the trauma in her life and accept herself as the lovely, talented person she had been all the time.

FACE IN THE MIRROR

I looked into the mirror and saw a stranger,
I longed to take her in my arms and hold her close;
She looked so lost, so sad,
as though there was some danger,
I wanted to assure her there was hope.

I smiled and held my arms out to her,
She smiled back and looked me in the face,
And then she put her arms around me
And heaved a sigh, a sigh of great relief.

We held on tight and wept and cried together
And spilled the pain and grief of long years past;
And when I looked once more at my reflection
The stranger had become my friend at last.

Clarifying confusion. Most victims of child sexual abuse are confused about what happened to them and why. One way to reduce the confusion is to learn as much as possible about sexual abuse. Reading the first part of this book will help you understand more about the nature and dynamics of abuse and those who perpetrate it. Additional books on the subject are listed in the resource section at the end of this book.

Talking to a counselor will help greatly. Your counselor might also help put you in touch with other victims of sexual abuse. Sharing experiences with others who have had the same type of trauma can be of immense help in clarifying your confusion.

To help estimate the amount of distress that might be impacting you as a result of child sexual abuse, the following circumstances can be considered:

☐ The distress is usually greater when the abuse involved physical violence as well as sexual abuse.

☐ The distress is greater when a child is abused by a trusted person or family member rather than by a stranger.

☐ The distress is less when the incidents of abuse are brief than when the abuse continues over a long period.

☐ The distress is less when the abuse takes place at a very young age in contrast to abuse when the child is older.

☐ Calm, supportive reactions from family members minimize the distress, while disorganized, fault-finding, and extreme responses from the family can create more distress.[2]

Another part of clearing up some of the confusion is to understand your feelings. Seldom do victims have all good or bad feelings toward their abusers, or toward the rest of their families. Go through your list of events and feelings and ask God to help you understand how they all fit together. You probably feel anger toward the abuser. What other unpleasant feelings do you have? It is perfectly normal to have hostile feelings toward someone who harmed you. The question is whether you choose to hang on to those resentments or to get rid of them. More will be said about that in the next chapter.

You may also have some pleasant feelings toward the abuser.

What are those positive feelings? And how do you feel toward the non-offending spouse or family members? Do you blame them? What other positive or negative feelings do you have? What about yourself? Sort through the various feelings of anger, shame, guilt, bitterness, fear, and distrust. On the other hand, look at the positive feelings you have about yourself. What are those feelings?

At this point, the goal is to discover you have a variety of mixed feelings about the many people and events in your life. Life is not simple. Everything does not fall into black and white categories. Part of your growth is being able to handle the ambivalence of conflicting feelings. Feelings are neither right nor wrong, but they do tell us how we are dealing with life. If you have spent years avoiding the feelings associated with your abuse, this has been a difficult part of the journey to recovery. Continue to be diligent in prayer and effort, as we go to the next chapter and examine the specific issues of anger, forgiveness, fear, shame, guilt, low self-esteem, and lack of trust.

NOTES

1. David A. Seamands, *Healing of Memories* (Wheaton, Ill.: Victor Books), 1985.
   H. Norman Wright, *Making Peace with Your Past* (Old Tappan, N.J.: Revell), 1985.
2. Adapted from Lynn B. Daugherty, *Why Me? Help for Victims of Child Sexual Abuse (Even If They Are Adults Now)* (Racine, Wis.: Mother Courage Press), 1984, pp. 59-60.

CHAPTER EIGHT

Overcoming the Pain

Ministering to the Needs of Adults Sexually Abused as Children

Attractive, in a hard sort of way, Teresa, age thirty-four, was telling her story. "My childhood was kind of rough. Mostly because my uncle and brother abused me. I was ten or eleven when my uncle started doing it. He would come into the house from next door when nobody was there. Often he was drunk. He'd chase me around and grab me, but there was nothing I could do. It went on for about a year before I told my mom about it. She didn't believe me 'cause it was her brother. I still can't believe my mom did that to me!

"Later, my older brother tried the same thing. I don't remember much about that. I guess I blocked the whole thing out. I remember staring at the ceiling and counting the holes in the plaster every time he did it to me.

"I've always had problems with men. My relationships always seem to go bad. I just can't seem to trust them. On the other hand, I haven't met one I should trust. They're only after one thing.

"I got good grades up until the sixth grade. Then I started

getting in trouble at school. I had a lot of social problems—getting into fights, not obeying the teachers, things like that. I especially had a tough time with men teachers. I suppose it had something to do with the abuse stuff. I didn't see it that way at the time though.

"I got married to a nice guy when I was twenty-three, but it has been up and down ever since the honeymoon. I just can't stand sex.

"I really feel alone and ugly. Life just doesn't make any sense to me. I get so mad sometimes I could shoot somebody. I used to go to church, but how could a loving God let all of that bad stuff happen to me?

"What do you think I should do?"

Teresa's experience previews the content of this chapter. We will look at the specific feelings of anger, fear, shame, guilt, low self-esteem, and inability to trust. With each topic, some practical suggestions will be given on how to deal with those feelings and come to terms with your abuse as a child.

LEARNING FROM YOUR ANGER

The first step in dealing with your anger is to recognize and admit you are feeling angry. Then you can decide what to do with it. There is nothing wrong with feeling anger. It's a danger signal. Anger is the feeling of displeasure or irritation that comes when we are interfered with, injured, or threatened. In its beginning stages, anger is the automatic response to perceived danger or threat. Feeling angry is not sinful. It is what we do with those angry feelings that may or may not get us into trouble.

Here are some ideas to help you identify and express your anger. If you are seeing a counselor, consult with him or her about the appropriateness of these activities.

Write a letter. Take your list of events and feelings surrounding the abuse and write a letter to the abuser. Ask God to reveal to you any hidden reaches of your memory, and thank Him that it is all right for you to deal with your feelings, however intense they may be. You will not ever send this letter. Do not worry about neatness, spelling, or style. You are just identifying, expressing, and draining your feelings. Because the letter is for your use only, it doesn't matter if the offender is dead or otherwise unavailable.

Pour all your anger into the letter. Don't hold back. Describe the terror, guilt, feelings of betrayal, and shame. Call the person all the angry names you wish. Tell the abuser how much he hurt you. Tell him how his exploitation of you for his own pleasure has affected your life. Don't judge your feelings as good or bad, right or wrong. The feelings are there and need to be expressed. If you have a tape recorder, you may want to use it instead of, or in addition to, the letter. Yell if you feel like it. Playing back the tape can help you realize the intensity of your feelings.

Read over your letter or play back the tape several times. Are there more angry things you would like to express? Go ahead and add them. Make sure you get down all the angry thoughts you've wished you could say. Stop and rest for a while. Take several days or weeks to reflect on the content and completeness of the letter.

If you come across angry feelings toward the non-offending parent or other family or community members, write a letter to each of them.

Read the letter. Now take your letter to a room with two chairs in it. Sit down and imagine the abuser is in the other chair. Read the letter as you imagine him listening to you, understanding your feelings, and accepting what you have to say. If additional feelings of hate, anxiety, fear, depression, or confusion arise, go ahead and amplify on what you have written. Don't imagine the abuser responding with a confession, requests for forgiveness, or grief for his wrongdoing. That is a choice he has to make, and you can't make him repent by this process. Your goal here is to establish an atmosphere for making a total disclosure of your feelings about the abuse.

Continue this process as long, or as often, as necessary—until all of your feelings have been shared. If you find yourself feeling emotionally drained, take a break. Go on to other tasks and come back at a later time.

The last step in the sequence is to invite Jesus into the scene. Close your eyes and visualize yourself, Jesus, and the abuser standing together in a peaceful setting. Imagine Christ's arms around the both of you. It may be premature to visualize any physical contact between you and the abuser, but Christ can be the link standing between you. You might imagine the abuser at least making a verbal acceptance of your feelings and statements.[1]

Repeat the process as necessary for any other people with whom you feel angry and resentful.

Visualize correspondence with the offender. Another use for your letter to the abuser is to imagine what he would be feeling as he opens the letter and starts reading it. Read the letter to yourself, but try to experience and understand the emotions and thoughts he might experience as he reads your letter. Now write a response to your letter as you think the abuser would answer. Try to be him as much as possible. Then prepare your answer to his response. Continue this correspondence with the abuser as long as it seems helpful. You might also repeat this exercise with the non-offending parent as the correspondent.[2]

Talk to someone. Another positive way to express your anger is to talk to a trusted person about your feelings. You are taking a risk because you don't know exactly how the friend will react, so do your best to find a caring person who is willing to listen. But it is a risk worth taking. The anger will not go away completely, but it will no longer be trapped inside.

Take part in some physical activity. Often anger needs a physical outlet. Vigorous physical activity can help reduce your intensity to the point you can think about things more clearly. Running, hitting a punching bag, beating a tennis racket on a pillow, chopping wood, throwing a tantrum, playing a competitive sport, swimming, or anything else that takes a lot of energy can help you vent your anger.

Feelings of anger often lead to a desire to seek revenge. This brings us to the major ingredient in coping with anger—forgiveness.

FORGIVENESS: THE KEY INGREDIENT

Forgiveness can be considered after, but not before, the extent of angry feelings are explored. There are four stages in the process of forgiving—hurt, hate, revenge, and relinquish. Each of these phases is important; *none should be skipped.*

1. *Recognize the hurt.* Forgiveness is an intellectual exercise unless the depths and extent of your hurt are known and explored. Forgiveness is necessary when someone has caused you unfair pain. You have been wronged by someone you trusted. An

accident may cause problems, but forgiveness is an issue only when a person makes a decision to cause harm or injustice, to treat you in a way you don't deserve. The unnecessary nature of the pain is what leads to the second stage, feelings of hate.

2. *Hate is a strong word, but an appropriate one, especially for victims of child sexual abuse.* Hate is a normal response to any deep and unfair pain. It is an instinctive backlash against anyone who hurts us by conscious choice. Hate tends to nurture the recall of the offense in such a way as to contaminate and block the relationship. It is very close to bitterness, which is an exasperated or provoked anger. While it is a natural human reaction to intentional pain, Scripture admonishes against maintaining this long-standing grudge (Ephesians 4:26, 31; James 3:14).

It doesn't help to pretend to be ignorant of the offense or to have forgotten the event. This gets us back to the denial that functions like a malignant growth or poison. The author of Hebrews gives us the "rotten apple" principle when he says, "See to it that no one misses the grace of God and that no bitter root grows up to cause trouble and defile many" (Hebrews 12:15). If bitterness is allowed to remain alongside your other feelings and thoughts, it will become like a rotten apple that ends up spoiling the whole barrel. A wife victimized as a child, while not responsible for the abuse, must be accountable for the bitterness that can create havoc in her current family relationships.

Peggy was abused by her brother and uncle during her preteen years. Because she hadn't acknowledged her feelings and dealt with them, she harbored a bitterness that contributed to problems in her sexual adjustment with her husband. It also caused Peggy to overeat and overspend as she sought ways to regain control over some aspect of her world. Eventually she confronted both abusers with satisfying results and found the bitterness to be far less of an issue in her life.

3. *Revenge is the goal of feelings of resentment.* Resentment is like charcoal embers—they may look gray and harmless, but to touch them would bring instant pain. Resentment is an enduring form of anger that desires to retaliate or seek revenge.

The principle of revenge or punishment is a natural part of God's order, as the Bible makes clear. "The wages of sin is death" (Romans 6:23). "It is Mine to avenge; I will repay. In due time their foot will slip; their day of disaster is near and their doom rushes upon them" (Deuteronomy 32:35). "For because of such things God's wrath comes on those who are disobedient" (Ephesians 5:6).

The major ingredient in being able to grant forgiveness is to satisfy the basic emotional requirement: *someone has to pay.* If you were abused by your stepfather, your natural response will be to want someone to pay for that pain and loss. A sin has been committed and you desire revenge! Of course, childhood will never be restored. You will not gain the ideal father you never had. And the memory of the abuse may never be completely washed away. But you want to be assured some legitimate sacrifice is paid by the one who committed the offense.

It's against this backdrop of a desire for payment that the death of Christ on the cross begins to take on new meaning. Many of my clients have experienced severe and lengthy abuse earlier in their lives. It was only when the substitutionary atonement of Jesus Christ was presented in a very practical manner that they were able to break free from the bondage of bitterness.

Isaiah 53:10-11 is a crucial passage in understanding the payment principle.

> *Yet it was the Lord's will to crush Him and cause Him to suffer*, and though the Lord makes His life a guilt offering, He will see His offspring and prolong His days, and the will of the Lord will prosper in His hand. After the *suffering of His soul, He will see the light of life, and be satisfied*; by His knowledge My righteous servant will justify many, and He will bear their iniquities (italics added).

Because God is just, and sin had to be punished, it was satisfying to God for the penalty of sin to be paid. It cost God His only Son. Death, the ultimate price for an offense, was paid by the One least likely to deserve it, the punishment for wrongdoing being handed down by the ultimate Judge, God Almighty.

It's at this point you can make an emotional break from the resentment and bitterness that come with the injustices inflicted upon you. Through the use of visualization, meditation on Scripture, and even symbolic action, the burden of anger and rage can be vented toward Christ's death on the cross.

4. *The final step in forgiveness is to relinquish your right to*

seek revenge. Forgiveness means to yield up the right to impose a penalty, to give away the right to judge someone despite the severity of his injustice.

There are two ways to deal with pain and frustration. Adding undisciplined anger to a traumatic situation results in bitterness. But if forgiveness is added to your initial pain, healing can result. What a difference! From victim to victor by relinquishing your right to judge the behavior of others.

Forgiveness includes awareness that the behavior of the abuser was definitely wrong. The healing comes by actively choosing to give up the desire to seek revenge or to impose and carry out the sentence. Forgiveness involves canceling a debt (Matthew 18:32-34). Forgetting is not a requirement. You may always be able to recall some aspects of your abusive history. But if forgiveness has taken place, the traumatic sting will be removed from those memories.

Forgiveness is an act of the will, not a result of feelings. Seldom will you *feel* like granting forgiveness to someone who has abused you, but that doesn't mean you should cover over those feelings. (That is why the first two stages of forgiveness dwelt on the facts of your hurt and hatred.) It's very important to acknowledge your bitterness and resentment. But you are not to stay fixed upon those feelings. The wrongdoing of your abuser does not entitle you to the sin of revenge or continued bitterness.

I have heard battered wives, or women abused by their fathers, report their rage and intense desire to hurt the one who had inflicted bodily harm and humiliation on them. While I can appreciate the source of the anger, the wounds will not be healed by their becoming the avenger.

Yes, somebody has to pay for the abuse you experienced. And that "Somebody" is Jesus Christ.

If you have had difficulty in removing your resentment about past hurts, try unloading the burden of anger and revenge on the thorn-scarred head of Jesus. As impossible as it may seem, take the perspective of God for a few moments. Place the source of your hatred on the cross with Christ. With all the imagination and feeling you can muster, direct your wrath in the direction of the cross. When your heart wants to strike out and physically injure your abuser, imagine the pain suggested by this verse: "But He was pierced for our transgressions, He was crushed for our

117

iniquities; the punishment that brought us peace was upon Him, and by His wounds we are healed" (Isaiah 53:5).

You can actually find pleasure, as God did, in the substitutionary death of Christ. Not in some morbid sense of seeing someone die on a cross, but in the sense of knowing justice has been served. A choice was made by your abuser that resulted in untold suffering for you, but the price of pain and death has been paid. At this point, you can be released from the burden of seeking your own revenge. Christ atoned for that person who offended you, and you can emerge the victor over bitterness!

Forgive yourself. Very often, victims of abuse struggle with the issue of forgiving themselves for participating in the abuse. I will talk about guilt more a bit later, but the ability to forgive yourself fits here. There are three aspects to forgiveness: (1) we are to ask God for forgiveness when we sin (1 John 1:9); (2) we are to ask forgiveness from others when we offend them (James 5:16); and (3) we are to grant forgiveness to others when they have sinned against us, even if they don't ask (Matthew 6:14-15; Ephesians 4:32; Colossians 3:13).

If you are obedient to these three requirements of forgiveness, then the ability to give up your own desire to see the abuser punished will be achieved. God has made us so that we are not able to accept His forgiveness unless we yield up our desire to extract penalties for the offenses committed against us. "Forgive us our sins, for we also forgive everyone who sins against us" (Luke 11:4). If we expect God to forgive us without imparting that same grace to others, we are being disobedient and the ability to forgive ourselves will be absent.

RECOGNIZING AND OVERCOMING FEAR

The first step in overcoming fear is to acknowledge it. Make a list of all of your fears that seem related to your abuse as a child. What do your dreams tell you about your fears? Add these ideas to your list.

After compiling the list, ask yourself which of your fears are realistic. The vast majority of our worries are over events that are insignificant, out of our control, water under the bridge, or yet to come. In what category do your fears fall?

Another helpful question is whether your fears or worries are resulting in growth in the intellectual, social, physical, emotional, or spiritual areas of your life. If growth isn't evident, it's time to make some changes.

As a child you may have developed a fearful nature because of the uncertain circumstances and the realistic prospect of further abuse over which you had very little control. This fear may have followed you into adulthood. While the immediate presence of harm is not evident, a generalized type of fear called anxiety may burden you. A counselor may be needed to help you overcome extensive feelings of anxiety and dread. The following ideas are drawn from a more extensive discussion of worry and anxiety in my book *Transformed By Thorns.*[3]

Anxiety is an internal conversation that makes absolutes out of possibilities. It is the tendency to place your trust in the likelihood of some improbable future event. The key to eliminating anxiety is to place your trust in ideas and events that are solid, predictable, and helpful for growth. God is interested in your growth and is faithful to help you overcome your fears. "The Lord is my light and my salvation—whom shall I fear? The Lord is the stronghold of my life—of whom shall I be afraid?" (Psalm 27:1)

Your own experience as a victim of abuse gives painful testimony to the risk of trusting in your own ability to prevent danger. The only solution is to place your trust in God. "Trust in the Lord with all your heart and lean not on your own understanding; in all your ways acknowledge Him, and He will make your paths straight" (Proverbs 3:5-6).

Faith demands that we choose to believe God is who He says He is and that He can deliver what He promises. Consider these promises:

☐ God cannot lie (Hebrews 6:18).
☐ He has never failed to keep His promises (1 Kings 8:56).
☐ He has guaranteed to be faithful (Deuteronomy 7:9; 1 Corinthians 1:9).
☐ He knows our limits (Isaiah 43:1-3; 1 Corinthians 10:13; 2 Peter 2:9).
☐ He will deliver us from afflictions (Psalm 30:5; 41:3).
☐ He will comfort us in hard times (Isaiah 43:2).
☐ His grace is sufficient for our weaknesses (2 Corinthians 12:9).

119

☐ He will take care of our bodily needs (Psalm 37:3).
☐ He will answer our prayers (Mark 11:24).
☐ He will help remove obstacles (Luke 17:6).
☐ He will give us spiritual fullness and light (John 6:35; 12:46).
☐ He will provide power for service (John 14:12).
☐ He will give us eternal life (John 3:14-15).

These are but a few of the many promises God has given to each believer. You can claim each of them. I know your life has included pain and suffering. I also don't pretend to know why everything happens the way it does. I do know that God doesn't promise to eliminate our problems in life. But He does promise to help us cope with those problems in such a way as to bring glory to His name. Believing and then acting on these promises assures even victims of abuse that the "God of peace will be with you" (Philippians 4:9).

God does heal our pain and erase our fears. But each of us must reach a point where we can say, "Lord, I am weak. My fear and anxiety are overwhelming. Come and fill my life with peace, that I may learn to rejoice in Your glory."

REMOVING THE SHAME

Victims of child sexual abuse feel different from other people. It may help to remember that you are not alone. The next time you go to church, a movie, or a concert, look around you. Count the number of people. Remember that one out of four women, and perhaps one out of eight or ten men, has been sexually abused. If there are 200 people in the building, that means there may be fifty other persons who were, or are now, victims of abuse! There are fifty other people who are just like you. You're not really so different after all.

Also, try to pick out those people who were abused. Look at the persons in your pew. If ten people are present, at least one of them, other than you, is also a victim. Can you tell who the victims are? Of course not. Victims can't be identified just by looking at them.

You may also feel people would not like you if they knew about the sexual abuse. And that is the sad truth in some cases. But there are some people who would not like you even if you hadn't been abused. They would base their opinion on the fact you are too tall or too short, too fat or too skinny, too old or too young. Some people wouldn't like you because of your skin color or because you live in a particular neighborhood. People develop dislikes for a million different reasons. Your abuse is only one possibility out of those millions.

Other adults have come from alcoholic or broken homes, families where crime was common, or grew up with a multitude of other problems. Before God, none of us can say we have lived a perfect life. We have all sinned and come short of the glory of God (Romans 3:23). There is no need to be any more ashamed of abuse in your life than any other misfortune. Continue thinking on how you are similar to others, not how you are different.

DEALING WITH GUILT

It was not your fault that you were chosen to be the victim of sexual abuse. You were available when the abuser, with no regard for your welfare, needed to fill his own needs. Remember that the total responsibility for the abuse lies with the abuser.

If a trusted person in a power position touches a child in a sexual way, it is not the child's responsibility to stop the abuse. Even if a child behaves in a manner interpreted as seductive by the father, she is not to blame. While it is normal for girls to act in ways that appear sexual to adults, it is not acceptable for their fathers to exploit them.

When the sexual abuse is disclosed, a crisis in the family often results. Many children assume this crisis is their fault and feel guilty for causing the upset. The perpetrators of child sexual abuse are usually older than their victims. Children have every right to expect safety, not abuse, from their caretakers. When a child is abused, he or she has the right to tell others of the incident. It is the abuser who must assume full responsibility for any disruption that takes place as a result of the disclosure.

Guilt may be fostered by such questions as, "Why did you let it happen? Why didn't you resist?" Sexual abuse of children usually follows such a subtle progression that boys and girls often don't even realize it is abnormal. If the abuser is skilled, force or threats are seldom necessary. Most victims cooperate. But this is one of the reasons why, later, they suffer so much guilt. Because children are taught to obey their parents, a child who is abused by her father has no real choice but to comply.

Another guilt-producer is the question, "Why didn't you tell?" Because there was no instruction about preventing abuse a generation ago, adults who were abused as children could not usually be expected to risk the consequences of telling. Fear keeps incest a family secret in many families. The child fears retaliation by the abuser or other family members. Threats or inducements to keep the secret may have been made. The child may have felt pressure to protect the mother or to keep the father from being sent away. These, and other pressures, take the responsibility away from the child.

Just because you *feel* guilty does not make it true. You can change the way you feel by changing the kinds of messages you tell yourself. If you tell yourself the abuse was all your fault, then you can expect to continue to feel guilty. Stop telling yourself lies. Say "Stop!" whenever a guilt-inducing thought enters your mind. Memorize some of the statements given in this section that apply to your particular situation. Then, whenever you have issued a "Stop" command to yourself, replace the untrue statement with a true one.

Perhaps you occasionally took advantage of the abuse. You may have used the abuse to gain special favors or lord your favored position over your brothers or sisters. If this happened, you may be dealing with true guilt. Confess that situation. Ask forgiveness. There is no reason why you should continue to punish yourself for mistakes of years ago.

BUILDING YOUR SELF-ESTEEM

Being a victim of abuse may have convinced you that you are worthless and that no one could ever care about you. Every person has both good and bad qualities. Each of us is important and worthwhile. Each of us can be loved and cherished by others and by ourselves.

The one who accepts her own self, who knows her strengths and weaknesses, and who can affirm herself as God affirms her has all she needs to maintain strong self-esteem. Look at the biblical evidence of your worth:

You were fearfully and wonderfully made (Psalm 139:13-16). You are the product of God's workmanship (Ephesians 2:10). You were created in the image of God. His likeness resides within you (Genesis 1:26). Furthermore, God likes what He sees in you (Genesis 1:31). He doesn't look at you, see your imperfections, and say, "I've made a mistake here. I'd better try again."

God values you enough that He seeks your worship (John 4:23). Christ, His Son, accepts you as you are—with no strings attached (John 6:37). You are precious in God's eyes (Isaiah 43:4). You are important enough to God that He allowed the spilling of the blood of His Son, Jesus Christ, for your benefit (1 Peter 1:18-19). Further, you have been adopted by God and made a son or daughter, like Jesus Christ Himself (Romans 8:14-17).

These are the *facts* of your value and importance to God. To overcome any doubt brought on by your abusive history, you need to *know* these facts.

The next crucial step is to *accept* the love God has given to you. For many, it is difficult to simply receive His gift. Many try to earn God's love by being extra good. Others try to qualify by suffering pain and doing penance. The truth is, all we have to do is accept what is freely given.

Numerous victims of child sexual abuse continue to tell themselves lies. They tend to only look at the bad and have trouble accepting the love of God, along with the love of those around them. When you find yourself dwelling on the negative, bring yourself back to these statements of God's value for your life.

LEARNING HOW TO TRUST

One of the major scars of child sexual abuse is the loss of the ability to trust. Because a person with a position of trust took advantage of your vulnerability, it has left an indelible mark of suspicion. There are no easy answers here. It may take a long time before you can learn to trust others again. Trusting someone will always involve a risk. Sometimes that risk will pay off and sometimes your trust will be betrayed. Remember, this happens to everybody, not just to victims of abuse.

It is also true that just because one or two people betrayed your trust, it doesn't mean everybody else will. Learn from your experiences. If you take the time, you will be able to find people who are worthy of your trust. Take yourself, for example. Are you trustworthy? Can you be counted on to keep your promises? Do you manipulate or victimize others? If you believe you can be trusted, there are surely other people just as reliable as you. Look for them. You are not the only one of your kind.

The more you can allow yourself to trust and find that risk rewarded, the more willing you will be to trust again. Success breeds success. Go slowly, but life is too lonely to go it alone.

A client struggled with the trauma of her abuse for many years. Depression was her constant companion for most of her adult life. After a particularly troublesome weekend, we talked again, and several key insights fell into place for her. Soon after, she penned the following lines. With her permission, I share them with you in the knowledge that you also can be made whole.

NO LONGER BROKEN

No longer broken
Made whole by God's grace.
No longer broken
There's joy in my face.
No longer broken
For God's made me whole
No longer broken
There's peace in my soul.

NOTES

1. Adapted from H. Norman Wright, *Making Peace with Your Past* (Old Tappan, N.J.: Revell), 1985, pp. 69-75.
2. Adapted from Henry Giarretto, *Integrated Treatment of Child Sexual Abuse* (Palo Alto, Calif.: Science and Behavior Books, Inc.), 1982, pp. 47-49.
3. Grant L. Martin, *Transformed By Thorns* (Wheaton, Ill.: Victor Books), 1985, pp. 95-116.

CHAPTER NINE

Partners in Pain

The Nature and Scope of Spouse Abuse

PORT ANGELES, Wash.—Some members of Grady Ray Young's Southern Baptist Church are incredulous. His children appear stunned.

Young, the 60-year-old preacher at Hillcrest Baptist Church, was charged yesterday in the slaying of his wife of 38 years.

Prosecutors say that Young used a .22-caliber rifle to kill his wife, Elva Mae, and then tried to pin it on a nonexistent burglar.

The bespectacled, frail-looking minister—wearing orange Clallam County overalls and tennis shoes with no socks—appeared before visiting Judge James Roper and formally was charged with the slaying last Saturday at their mobile home, about 100 yards from the church.[1]

The guilt of Pastor Young was not yet determined at the time of this news article, but the story illustrates the fact that a spouse killing a spouse accounts for 15 to 20 percent of all murders committed in the United States. Recent figures from the U.S.

Justice Department tell us 4,600 homicides a year occurred within the family. One fourth of those murders took place inside the home.

The FBI estimates that a wife is beaten every thirty seconds in this country. This totals 2,880 women who are beaten every day; over 1 million every year.[2] A recent journal article reports that one in ten women will be seriously beaten in the course of her marriage.

One of every twelve spouses commits at least one violent act against his or her partner every year. As many as 28 percent of all couples will engage in some form of physical abuse during their marriages.

Nor is spouse abuse limited to families outside the church. A national survey completed by the Center for the Prevention of Sexual and Domestic Violence in Seattle, Washington found that the typical parish clergy sees almost fourteen people each year who come with problems involving family violence.[3]

The United Methodist Church polled a sample of its membership and found that 68 percent of those questioned had personally experienced some type of family violence. This included child abuse, child sexual abuse, as well as spouse abuse.

Surprisingly, violence during courtship is as pervasive as violence within marriage. Statistics vary, but 14 to 49 percent of people dating are beaten, slapped, kicked, punched, or more seriously injured with knives or guns *before* they are married.[4] One wonders why they go ahead and marry, but they do.

While the vast majority of victims are women, some evidence exists that men are also abused. The problem is differentiating when the wife is the aggressor and when it is a simultaneous blowup, retaliation, or self-defense. One study estimated approximately 3.5 million women and 250,000 men are battered each year by their spouse or intimate partner.[5]

Most of the evidence, at this time, suggests men are seldom the victims of battering. When the male *is* abused, his injuries seem almost insignificant when compared to the more frequent and severe damage inflicted on women. Because of the more extensive incidence of abuse toward women, this discussion will concentrate on the female victim.

If you are a victim of spouse abuse, you don't need statistics to confirm your pain and agony. You may face daily the kind of anguish described in the words of David from Psalm 55:

> My heart is in anguish within me; the terrors of death assail me. Fear and trembling have beset me; horror has over-whelmed me. I said, "Oh, that I had the wings of a dove! I would fly away and be at rest—I would flee far away and stay in the desert; I would hurry to my place of shelter, far from the tempest and storm." . . . If an enemy were insulting me, I could endure it; if a foe were raising himself against me, I could hide from him. But it is you, a man like myself, my companion, my close friend, with whom I once enjoyed sweet fellowship as we walked with the throng at the house of God. . . . My companion attacks his friends; he violates his covenant. His speech is smooth as butter, yet war is in his heart; his words are more soothing than oil, yet they are drawn swords (Psalm 55:4-8, 12-14, 20-21).

A BRIEF HISTORY OF WIFE BEATING[6]

For centuries, wife beating has been accepted as a natural result of a woman's status as her husband's property. For much of our history, violence toward women has been socially, legally, and religiously endorsed. For generations, the husband was not just head of the household—he *was* the household.

Roman law gave the father the absolute right to sell his children as well as lifelong authority over all members of the household. In ancient Greece the order of family priority was: father, cattle, mother, children. No wonder violence toward wives was common. Broken-down old cows had more status than women.

The Jewish tradition was equally biased. A Jewish man prayed daily: "I thank God that He did not make me a Gentile, a slave, or a woman." Jewish law was permeated by the precept that a woman was not a person. She was her husband's possession, and he was free to do anything with her he pleased.

The Jewish divorce laws also reflected this inequality. The wife could not divorce her husband unless he became a leper, an apostate, or engaged in a "disgusting trade." A Jewish man, on the other hand, could divorce his wife for almost any reason. All he had to do was hand his wife a bill of divorce in the presence of

Please Don't Hurt Me

two witnesses and the marriage was ended.

This makes the Apostle Paul's statement in Galatians 3:28 so revolutionary: "There is neither Jew nor Greek, slave nor free, male nor female, for you are all one in Christ Jesus."

The Medieval Church frequently taught that a husband had the right, and sometimes even the obligation, to beat his wife. An example is found in Friar Cherubino's "Rules of Marriage." He states that if a husband's verbal correction of his wife was not effective, then he was to "take up a stick and beat her, not in rage, but out of charity and concern for her soul, so that the beating will rebound to your merit and her good."[7]

For the most part, medieval society viewed women as needing strict control. Here is an excerpt from one of the "marriage enrichment" manuals of that time. "The female is an empty thing, easily swayed: she runs great risks when she is away from her husband. Therefore, keep females in the house, keep them as close to you as you can, and come home often to keep an eye on your affairs and to keep them in fear and trembling. . . . If you have a female child, set her to sewing and not to reading, for it is not suitable for a female to know how to read unless she is going to be a nun."[8]

The Renaissance and Reformation brought significant social, political, and religious change. The Elizabethan wife was a curious mixture of slave and companion, a necessary evil, and a valued lieutenant. According to custom, a wife's primary duty was to be subject to her husband. She was always to acknowledge herself as an inferior being and be at the beck and call of her spouse.[9]

Permissiveness toward the striking of women became part of the American tradition, since the colonies borrowed much from English law. For example, the common colloquial expression *rule of thumb* originated from a section of British Common Law intended to regulate wife beating. The law was drafted to help the plight of abused women by modifying the weapons a husband could legally use when chastising his wife. The old law had authorized a husband to chastise her with any "reasonable" instrument. The new law stipulated the reasonable instrument be only "a rod not thicker than his thumb."[10]

For many years the battering of women was assumed and accepted as a male's right in American society. By the 1870s, however, the pendulum of punishment began to swing the other

128

way. States such as Massachusetts and Alabama began to reject the legal justification for wife beating. In Maryland, by 1882 a wife-beater could receive forty lashes or one year in prison. In Delaware, wife beating was punishable with five to thirty lashes at the whipping post. And in New Mexico, the crime carried a fine of $225 to $1,000, or one to five years in prison.[11]

By 1910, only eleven states still did not permit divorce by reason of cruelty within the marriage.

This brief review highlights the centuries of social, political, and religious tradition that has perpetuated violence toward women. The statistics quoted at the beginning of this chapter only serve to document a phenomenon that has been present for centuries.

DEFINITION OF SPOUSE ABUSE

Spouse abuse refers to brutal and intentional rather than to accidental or insubstantial physical contact. *Physical violence* includes any act or behavior that inflicts bodily harm or that is intended to do so. Physical violence may consist of kicking, hitting, shoving, choking, throwing objects, or using a weapon. The severity of physical assaults may range from a slap across the face to murder.

Emotional abuse may include ridiculing or demeaning statements, withholding affection or privileges, or blaming one's spouse for family or interpersonal problems. Emotional abuse often occurs in conjunction with physical violence, but it can occur by itself. Physical abuse leaves broken bones or bruises as evidence, while the consequences of emotional abuse are lowered self-esteem and feelings of helplessness.

Threatened violence is a type of emotional abuse. It can include verbal threats to harm, wielding of weapons, threatening gestures, injury or killing of family pets, destruction of property, or any other intimidating verbal or nonverbal behavior. Even if the threatened violence is not carried out, the apprehension and uncertainty may be more damaging to the victim than the physical act itself.

Marital rape is a form of sexual abuse where an unwilling partner is forced to participate in intercourse or other sexual acts against her will. It is often accompanied by physical abuse, or at least threats of harm.

129

WHERE AND WHEN DOES MARITAL VIOLENCE OCCUR?

We now know quite a bit about the context of marital violence. The following list summarizes some of that information.

- [ ] The usual location for marital violence is in the home, especially the living room or bedroom.
- [ ] The bedroom is the most likely place for a female to be killed. The conflict often occurs at night, when there is no place to go.
- [ ] The bathroom is the most frequently occupied room during domestic violence. The bathroom is the demilitarized zone of the home and typically is the one room in the house that always has a lock. Often this room is used as a refuge for family members to avoid violence.
- [ ] Marital couples most often engage in physical conflict between 6 P.M. and midnight.
- [ ] Marital violence is more frequent when neither spouse works, or when they work on alternating shifts.
- [ ] The evening meal is a particularly dangerous time due to the accumulation of daily frustrations. The wife complains about the children; the husband, about his work; and the children yell, cry, fight, or spill their milk.
- [ ] The conflict is most likely to begin over management of the children, with disagreements over money as the second most frequently cited cause.
- [ ] Weekends are more conducive to domestic violence than weekdays.
- [ ] Holidays such as Christmas or New Year's Eve are notable trouble times.
- [ ] There is a slight tendency for more violence to occur during the warm summer months.
- [ ] Violence is more likely to occur when the wife is pregnant.
- [ ] As the frequency of battering episodes increases, the more severe they become.[12]

PHASES IN MARITAL VIOLENCE

Tim and Kirstin were too young to get married in the first place. They had come together, in part, out of a need to get away from the fighting in their own families. The first few months went just fine, but then their bills began to pile up. Kirstin kept asking Tim if she should go to work to help out, but he told her things would eventually work out. "Besides," he said, "I want you home. I don't think it's the woman's place to work. There are too many men out there looking for an easy mark."

She tried to be positive, but Kirstin could feel the tension building. Tim became more sullen and angry with each new frustration.

Knowing Tim was upset, Kirstin tried very hard to make him happy. One evening after fixing Tim's favorite dinner, Kirstin mentioned that a creditor had called about a past-due bill. Tim exploded, throwing his glass across the room. He raged on and on about every fault or mistake Kirstin had ever made. He even grabbed her arms and shook her. She was totally devastated by his attack and spent the evening crying in the bedroom.

A few hours later Tim came into the room and apologized, tears running down his face. "I don't know what came over me," he said. "Things haven't been working out the way I expected. Somehow I just can't handle it when I know you're disappointed in me. Things will be better. Just wait and see. I'll never yell at you again."

They fell into each other's arms and seemed closer than they ever had before.

Tim and Kirstin illustrate the early phases of the abusive cycle. There is a predictable progression of events that seem to repeat themselves again and again in an abusive relationship. One researcher has identified three distinct phases: (1) the tension-building phase; (2) the explosion; and (3) the remorse phase.[13]

Phase One: tension building. Irritations gradually escalate over such things as finances or children. Verbal complaints may surface, but the frustrations are not dealt with directly. Instead, the feelings are held inside where they become more intense. Communication and cooperation diminish as the couple, like Tim and Kirstin, tend to withdraw from each other. The batterer may express dissatisfaction and hostility but not in an extreme form. The wife may attempt to placate her husband, trying to please him, calm him down, and avoid further confrontations. The wife, at this point, tries not to respond to her husband's hostile actions. She tends to use some type of anger reduction technique, which often works for a little while. This temporary lull reinforces her belief that she can control her husband or prevent things from getting worse.

The tension will continue to increase and the wife eventually finds she is unable to control her husband's angry responses. Then she usually withdraws from her husband, not wanting to make things worse. The husband sees her withdrawal and reacts with more intense anger. The second phase becomes inevitable unless some type of intervention takes place. Sometimes the wife will precipitate the inevitable explosion so she can at least control where and when it occurs. This allows her to take better precautions to minimize her injuries and pain. The husband may also get drunk, anticipating a violent confrontation. Phase One may last anywhere from an hour to several months.

Phase Two: the acute violent episode. Like Tim's outburst, this phase is characterized by the uncontrollable discharge of tensions that have built up during Phase One. Prior to this episode of violence, there is often the feeling that an outburst is inevitable, that the situation is beyond either spouse's control. This is when the batterer unleashes his aggressive behavior toward his wife. If injuries occur, this is when they are inflicted.

Phase Two ends when the battering stops. With that action comes a reduction in tension. Tim's temper tantrum resulted in Kirstin dropping the subject of bill-paying. She fled the room and, by doing so, gave Tim a short-lived reprieve. Tim's violent behavior is reinforced, and he is likely to use it again in the future, because it worked.

Sometimes, just before the violence occurs, the husband may withdraw and refuse to communicate. Recall how Tim became more sullen and irritable over the course of several months. The man often does this because he can't compete with the verbal, argumentative skills of his wife. His retreat is motivated by frustration. He may then signal to her he is about to "lose it" and demand that his wife "back off." The example of Tim and Kirstin did not have this component because it was early in their marriage. After the cycle has been repeated a few times, Kirstin will be better able to anticipate Tim's outburst. She may then increase her efforts to get through to him by talking louder, moving closer, or preventing him from leaving. This intensifies the tension and violence erupts. In this case, both husband and wife feel victimized. The husband believes he was provoked into retaliation in the only way he knows how. The wife ends up being the obvious victim of physical and/or verbal attack.

Phase Three: remorse. After the explosive release of violence comes a period of relative calm. The tension has been dissipated—at least until it happens again. Tim apologized profusely to Kirstin. The abusive husband may also try to help his wife, show kindness and remorse, and shower her with gifts and promises that it will never happen again. This behavior often comes out of a genuine sense of guilt over the harm inflicted as well as of fear of losing his spouse. The husband, like Tim, may really believe he will never allow himself to be violent again. The wife wants very much to believe her husband and, for a time, may renew her hope in his ability to change.

The level of intimacy during this "make up" phase may be better than any other period in the lives of the couple. Tim and Kirstin had never felt the same intensity of emotions as were present during their time of reconciliation. A couple may communicate feelings in the context of guilt and vulnerability that usually don't get revealed.

A shift in power also may occur during this phase. The wife may now feel protective of her repentant husband because she is the stronger of the two. She now has gone from being comparatively powerless to powerful. If she were to make any threats or efforts to leave, the balance of power would be even more evident. The wife may try to punish her husband or obtain concessions and privileges. This may be satisfying for a while. But once the husband feels more secure about his wife staying with him, or after stressors reaccumulate, he will resent his loss of power, and the abusive cycle will start all over again.

CHARACTERISTICS OF MEN WHO BATTER[14]
Abusive men are found among all races, socioeconomic classes, and occupations. Some go to church and just as many do not. Some enduring qualities have been found among groups of men who batter. The following discussion will summarize the most common features.

1. *Problems with anger.* Abusive men are unable to manage their own anger nor can they deal with their wife's anger. They tend to either have a quick temper which often discharges, or a passive, sullen manner which allows anger to build up over time and then explode.

Most men who batter come from abusive backgrounds. Men who have experienced violent and abusive childhoods are more likely to grow up and become child and/or spouse abusers. If a man either observed his parents abusing each other or if he was abused as a child, he is more likely to use violence as the primary means for solving conflict.

2. *Inability to share feelings.* Abusive males have an especially hard time expressing their emotions as well as identifying and handling those feelings. This type of man is rarely capable of true intimacy and may feel very threatened by the prospect of being open and vulnerable.

Though many of these men have sufficient verbal skills to function in day-to-day living, they do not have the verbal ability to express what they think or feel. The abusive male expects instant gratification from his wife, who is expected to read his mind and "know" what her mate wants. When she is unable to do so, the husband may interpret this as meaning she does not really love him. He reacts to this "rejection" with violence.

3. *Emotional dependence and lack of friends.* Men who abuse their spouses are usually very emotionally dependent on their wives, and tend to be very jealous and possessive of them. This jealousy is usually sexual in nature. The man will frequently accuse his wife of sexual relations with others, often with family and friends.

He will almost paranoically monitor his spouse's activities and make accusations. Perhaps he might time how long it takes to go from the house to the grocery store, then call his wife to make sure she didn't meet her boyfriend on the way.

Abusive men have very few close friends and maintain only superficial contact with persons outside their own family.

Another sign of dependency is a husband making extraordinary attempts to persuade his wife to return after she has left him. The wife may find herself besieged with phone calls, letters, unwanted gifts, or middle-of-the-night visits from her husband. He may claim that he cannot live without her and will promise to make any changes necessary to get her back. Some will threaten suicide, though very few actually carry out this threat.

4. *Low self-esteem and lack of assertiveness.* Abusive men are generally nonassertive outside the home, possess low self-esteem, and are depressed. Since many abusive men come from violent backgrounds, it's easy to understand how hard it would be for one to reach adulthood with his self-image intact. The lack of self-esteem, combined with a history of hurt and fear, is quickly converted to anger and then aggression.

Depression can result from internalized anger, so it is very possible for some abusive men to ricochet between depressed nonassertiveness and aggression. Sometimes the aggression will spread outside the home and abusive men will lose their friends and jobs as a result. Many times the depression will be hidden under a macho exterior.

Lack of assertiveness means the inability to take initiative to openly express one's needs without coercion. Unassertiveness may result from the cultural stereotypes of masculinity which reinforce aggressive behavior. As a result, abusive males may resort to violence rather than verbal communication as a means to build their own masculine self-image.

5. *Rigid application of traditional sex roles.* Violent men tend to have more inflexible beliefs about the role and function of women. Many batterers are very dominating. They demand control of almost every aspect of their families. They expect to make all major decisions and tend to become angry if their wives disagree or act independently. Often the abusive husband tries to monitor his wife's activities outside the home, such as refusing to let her go to college or church.

Using his religious beliefs for support, the man who beats his wife tends to adhere to a male dominant role which requires that he: (1) never appears weak; (2) can solve his problems without asking for help; (3) make all important family decisions; (4) receive deferential treatment from his wife and children; and (5) be in control of his emotions, particularly in public.

He wants his wife to be responsible for all household and mothering chores and to be submissive and subservient. Because he is already insecure, the most innocuous of actions may be seen as a threat to his status as head of the family. For example, he might hit his wife because she drank the last can of pop.

6. *Alcohol and drug dependency.* Men who abuse their partners often have a problem with substance abuse. Alcohol abuse is more prevalent than drug abuse, and it is also likely to result in more serious injuries to women.

Though some form of substance abuse is often present in abusive relationships, this does not mean that drug or alcohol abuse is necessarily causing the violence. The use of alcohol and drugs may just allow the abuser to avoid responsibility for his behavior. It is likely substance abuse and marital violence are related, in that both problems represent an inappropriate response to stress.

7. *Financial and other problems.* Economic stressors such as unemployment, underemployment, or high levels of job dissatisfaction can be related to marital violence. The majority of abusers are working at the time of the violence, so stress from unemployment is even more of an excuse to hit, rather than merely being a cause-and-effect relationship.

The husband's sense of power at home is often related to how much power he has at work. Consequently, when abusive males feel threatened in their role as provider, and thus believe they are losing their power, they may resort to violence as an alternative means for expressing their authority in the family.

Any major event that would serve to upset the individual or family equilibrium, such as medical problems, discipline concerns, or pregnancy can certainly lead to violence.

8. *Social isolation.* Social isolation raises the risk that severe violence could occur between spouses. Physical isolation can also contribute, since access to social service agencies, medical or educational help, and family or friends may be limited. Families experiencing violence are usually unable to utilize the resources necessary to cope with their particular problems.

Most people who undergo stress are able to turn to other family members, friends, neighbors, or their church for financial and emotional support. Many abusive couples lack such a network. This isolation may be the result of frequent moves which were made to search for work, escape creditors, or to avoid social service intervention. Isolation can also be self-induced because either the abused woman or her husband is fearful the problem will become known by others.

CHARACTERISTICS OF BATTERED WOMEN[15]

One in ten women will be seriously assaulted by her husband sometime during the course of her marriage. It will happen again and again to at least one in twenty wives. Those who finally press charges will have been attacked an average of thirty-five times.[16]

Reasons vary why these women stay in such a painful situation. The following descriptions attempt to sketch a composite picture of the battered wife.

Battered women enter marriage with the same desires and goals as other women. They may tend to be somewhat more tolerant of physical aggression because they are likely to have come from homes with a history of violence.

The initial episodes of violence typically begin during the first year of marriage. In the beginning, the woman tends to blame herself. She thinks that if she had acted differently her spouse might not have resorted to physical violence. Because the husband is usually remorseful, the wife may try to excuse his behavior. Her belief in the excuses dissolves, however, as the assaults occur more often and become more severe. Quite often, by the time the wife realizes the beatings are a dangerous and permanent part of her marriage, she feels paralyzed to take action.

1. *Low self-esteem.* A battered woman is likely to have grown up with self-esteem problems. This lack of self-worth makes her vulnerable to her husband's verbal and physical abuse. As the emotional abuse increases, it's hard for the woman not to believe her husband's ridicule. Eventually she may conclude that she does not deserve anything better and may give up any attempts to improve the situation. When her husband tells her, "You ought to be thankful I keep you around, because no one else would have you," she is likely to inwardly accept what he says, especially if no one else is around to contradict his statement.

The battered wife tends to put everybody else's needs before her own. She will make many personal and emotional sacrifices to meet the needs of her husband and children; indeed she may even burn herself out trying to please her family. The battered wife will tend to take on the guilt for her husband's abusive behavior. Her focus will be on what *she* can do to make the violence stop, without major consideration of her *husband's* responsibility.

2. *Unrealistic hope.* Most abused women value their marriages

137

and are intensively involved with their husbands. Despite the pain they suffer, they still feel love and loyalty for their mates. The abused wife feels responsible for her husband and believes he needs her. Many battered wives are rescuers. They believe if they hang in there long enough, eventually their husbands will change for the better. That may have even been one of the reasons they married men with problems in the first place.

Time and time again the abusive husband will promise to change, and the wife clings to this eternal hope because she wants to believe it. Besides, the wife often enjoys the relationship when abuse is not occurring. During those periods, the man may be a good father and an affectionate husband.

Another aspect that draws an abused woman back to the vicious cycle of hurt is a process of traumatic bonding. After a beating, the woman is exhausted and in pain. She feels both vulnerable and dependent. Her husband is likely to feel guilty and will try to make things better by being especially loving and kind. The wife accepts his comfort because she has no other options. At this point, the battered woman bonds to the warmer side of her husband because he still meets some of her needs to be loved.

3. *Isolation.* Another characteristic of battered women is gradual social isolation. Often, by the time a battered wife comes for help, she has cut off most of her family and friends. Her husband prefers that she stay at home, so her social network is reduced. Sometimes her isolation is self-imposed because she fears her family and friends will find out about the abuse. Fear also plays a part, because the wife doesn't want any retaliation against anyone who might find out about the situation and incur the wrath of her husband.

Isolation tends to perpetuate ignorance of resources designed to deal with abuse. The battered wife becomes even more bonded into the abusive relationship, because she believes there are no alternatives for help or protection.

4. *Emotional and economic dependency.* The battered wife is very reliant on her husband, especially financially. She may not have the skills, education, or experience to obtain help for her situation. Even if the battered wife is working, there is a strong chance her husband still controls the money.

What's more, many abused women have very little self-confidence after years of abuse. They are apt to show a sense of helplessness far below their potential for coping. They find security in the familiar. The prospect of making a change involves too much risk. They don't want to be alone outside the confines of the destructive relationship, even though their marriage is lonely and isolated.

Abused women often will come for help only when they believe their children are in danger. Emergency-room personnel report that abused women only show up for treatment when there is blood. The sight of blood seems to trigger a realization that personal danger is involved. Even if internal injuries or broken bones result, many abused wives will not go to the hospital. They have lost touch with their physical boundaries, which includes the awareness of pain.

5. *Traditional view of marriage.* Most battered women, whether Christian or not, try to fulfill a traditional role in marriage. They see themselves primarily as wives and mothers who should be nurturing, submissive, and forgiving of their spouses' failures. If the marriage is not satisfying, they are the ones responsible to make it better. An abused wife tends to view the degree of success in her marriage as a reflection of her own worth. Therefore, if the marriage is not successful, she is failing as a person as well as a wife and mother.

If raised in a broken home, the abused wife may not want to "fail" as her parents did. Cultural or religious constraints regarding separation or divorce may deter her from seeking help. Fear of physical retaliation, economic reversal, or loss of custody of children can also create a paralysis that keeps an abused wife locked in a bad situation.

* * * * *

This concludes the discussion of the nature and scope of wife abuse, and the characteristics of both the abuser and the victim. The next two chapters will deal with how to cope with the actual crisis of spouse abuse and how to work toward recovery.

NOTES

1. Don Duncan, "Grief, Disbelief in Port Angeles," *The Seattle Times,* August 14, 1986, A 1.

2. William A. Stacey and Anson Shupe, *The Family Secret* (Boston: Beacon Press), 1983, pp. 2-3.
3. Marie Fortune, "The Church and Domestic Violence," in *Theology: News and Notes,* Fuller Theological Seminary, June, 1982, p. 17.
4. Jamie Talan, "Studies Find Premarital Violence High," *The Seattle Times,* November 29, 1985, G 1.
5. S.K. Steinmetz, *The Cycle of Violence: Assertive Aggressive and Abusive Family Interaction* (New York: Preger Publishers), 1977, p. xvii.
   S.K. Steinmetz, "The Battered Husband Syndrome" in *Victimology: An International Journal,* vol. 2 (3-4), 1977-78, pp. 499-509.
6. The following material adapted from Grant L. Martin, *Counseling for Family Violence and Abuse* (Waco, Texas: Word), 1987, pp. 22-26.
7. Julia O'Faolain and Lauro Martines, eds., *Not in God's Image* (New York: Harper & Row), 1973, p. 177.
8. Ibid. p. 169.
9. Carroll Camden, *The Elizabethan Woman* (Houston: Elsevier Press), 1952, p. 148.
10. Terry Davidson, "Wifebeating: A Recurring Phenomenon Throughout History," in *Battered Women: A Psychosociological Study of Domestic Violence,* Maria Roy, ed. (New York: Van Nostrand Reinhold), 1977, p. 14.
11. Elizabeth Pleck, "Wife Beating in Nineteenth-Century America," in *Victimology: An International Journal,* vol. 4 (1), 1979, p. 61.
12. Grant L. Martin, *Counseling for Family Violence and Abuse* (Waco, Texas: Word), 1987, p. 12.
13. Lenore E. Walker, *The Battered Woman Syndrome* (New York: Springer), 1984, pp. 95-104.
14. The following material adapted from Grant L. Martin, *Counseling for Family Violence and Abuse* (Waco, Texas: Word), 1987, pp. 31-38.
15. Ibid., pp. 38-43.
16. E. Carpenter, "Traumatic Bonding and the Battered Wife," in *Psychology Today,* June 1985, p. 16.

CHAPTER TEN

Stopping the Violence

Ending the Pain of Spouse Abuse

Remember Tim and Kirstin who were introduced in chapter 9? Let's jump ahead about five years into their marriage and see what developed.

> It was 10 P.M. and Kirstin was sitting at the kitchen table overwhelmed with pain and fear. Every bone in her body ached. Her arms were bruised and one eye was almost swollen shut. Tim had just left in the car after another one of the "family squabbles," as he called them.
>
> "Everybody has their differences," Tim would often say. "We just have more than some."
>
> "More than some," wasn't her only concern. Over the past several years Kirstin had been battered so many times she lost count. The pattern that had its beginning five years ago continued to haunt their marriage. Tim had lost and quit many different jobs. They had moved from one location to another, trying to avoid bill collectors, or to "make a new start," as Tim would say.
>
> Even with a new location, and the accompanying prom-

ises, Tim's anger would eventually surface, and Kirstin would end up being the punching bag. There had been some good times. Tim was a good father to Tommy and Cammie. But the children were seeing all this turmoil, and Kirstin knew it had to stop. The problem was she didn't know what to do or where to turn. She couldn't leave Tim. She had nowhere to go, there was no money, and she had no skills to get a decent job. As far as she could tell, there didn't seem to be any way out.

Maybe you can identify with Kirstin. You have experienced the pain and hopelessness of family violence. You want things to improve, but don't know where to begin. If you are the victim of spouse abuse, or are concerned for someone who is, this chapter is for you. In chapter 9, you read about the general patterns in wife battering. Now we will examine specific options to bring about change.

Kirstin's situation will be used to illustrate some of the steps in setting priorities and sorting through the alternatives to get the battering to stop.

HOW TO BEGIN?
Most victims of spouse abuse feel totally helpless and have no idea where to begin. The following approach is suggested:

1. Take inventory of your situation.
2. Assess the level of harm and danger to yourself and others.
3. Explore your alternatives and resources for getting the abuse to stop.
4. Develop a safety plan with your welfare in mind.
5. Implement the plan as soon as possible.
6. Once you are safe, begin thinking about long-term alternatives.

TAKE INVENTORY
It is difficult to be reasonably objective about your situation. Many victims of wife abuse have become so numb to their

husbands' verbal and physical attacks that they lose contact with what is normal. You may have difficulty getting outside yourself long enough to see that the treatment you have been receiving does not have to be accepted as "your lot in life." Give yourself permission to consider a better way. You have a right to expect safety within your own home!

If you haven't done so already, read chapter 9 of this book. It gives an overview of spouse abuse—what it is; how often, where, and how it occurs; and the characteristics of both the abusive husband and the battered wife.

As you read that material, compare your experience to the examples and characteristics described there. How do you compare? If many similarities exist, you can begin to understand that wife battering is not only an inappropriate and abnormal form of behavior, but a crime that is hazardous to your health!

ASSESS THE LEVEL OF DANGER
To assist you in taking inventory as well as determining the level of danger, the questionnaire on pages 143-147 is included. The Abuse Index allows you, a friend, or relative of a victim, to estimate the degree of abuse. The results, if answered honestly, provide an objective picture of your situation.

CSR ABUSE INDEX[1]

Are You in an Abusive Situation?

This questionnaire is designed to help you decide if you are living in an abusive situation. There are different forms of abuse, and not every woman experiences all of them. Following are various questions about your relationship with a man. As you can see, each possible answer has points assigned to it. By answering each question and then totaling the points as directed, you can compare your score with the Abuse Index and evaluate if you are living in a potentially violent situation. And if you are abused, you will have some estimate of how really dangerous that abuse is.

143

Directions: Circle the response to each question that best describes your relationship.

	Fre-quently	Some-times	Rarely	Never
1. Does he continually monitor your time and make you account for every minute (when you run errands, visit friends, commute to work, etc.)?	3	2	1	0
2. Does he ever accuse you of having affairs with other men or act suspicious that you are?	3	2	1	0
3. Is he ever rude to your friends?	3	2	1	0
4. Does he ever discourage you from starting friendships with other women?	3	2	1	0
5. Do you ever feel isolated and alone, as if there was nobody close to you to confide in?	3	2	1	0
6. Is he overly critical of daily things, such as your cooking, your clothes, or your appearance?	3	2	1	0
7. Does he demand a strict account of how you spend money?	3	2	1	0
8. Do his moods change radically, from very calm to very angry, or vice versa?	3	2	1	0

9. Is he disturbed by you working or by the thought of you working?	3	2	1	0
10. Does he become angry more easily if he drinks?	3	2	1	0
11. Does he pressure you for sex much more often than you'd like?	3	2	1	0
12. Does he become angry if you don't want to go along with his requests for sex?	3	2	1	0
13. Do you quarrel much over financial matters?	3	2	1	0
14. Do you quarrel much about having children or raising them?	3	2	1	0
15. Does he ever strike you with his hands or feet (slap, punch, kick, etc.)?	6	5	4	0
16. Does he ever strike you with an object?	6	5	4	0
17. Does he ever threaten you with a household object or weapon?	6	5	4	0
18. Has he ever threatened to kill either himself or you?	6	5	4	0
19. Does he ever give you visible injuries (such as welts, bruises, cuts, lumps on the head)?	6	5	4	0

20. Have you ever had to treat any injuries from his violence with first aid? 6 5 4 0

21. Have you ever had to seek professional aid for any injury at a medical clinic, doctor's office, or hospital emergency room? 6 5 4 0

22. Does he ever hurt you sexually or make you have intercourse against your will? 6 5 4 0

23. Is he ever violent toward children? 6 5 4 0

24. Is he ever violent toward other people outside your home and family? 6 5 4 0

25. Does he ever throw objects or break things when he is angry? 6 5 4 0

26. Has he ever been in trouble with the police? 6 5 4 0

27. Have you ever called the police or tried to call them because you felt you or other members of your family were in danger? 6 5 4 0

TOTAL SCORE _____

Scoring: To score your responses, simply add up the points following each question. The sum of the twenty-seven items is your Abuse Index Score. To get some idea of how abusive your relationship is, compare your Index Score with the following chart.

120-94   Dangerously abusive
93-37   Seriously abusive
36-15   Moderately abusive
14-0   Nonabusive

If your score was in the 0-14 range, you live in a safe, nonabusive relationship. A score in the 15-36 range suggests you have experienced some violence, at least once in a while. There is no immediate problem, but watch out for any escalation of violence.

If your score is in the 37-93 range, you are in a seriously abusive situation. It is likely you have been injured already, and the prospect of future injury is also high. Things can become very dangerous if additional pressures come into your family. You would be strongly advised to seek help.

Scores in the top range of 94-120 represent serious jeopardy. You are most certainly in danger, and should take immediate steps to find safety. The violence is not miraculously going away. Your life, and possibly the welfare of your children, is at risk!

If Kirstin were to take the Abuse Index her score would be in the 50s—a seriously abusive situation. She had been injured numerous times, and the frequency and intensity of the abuse were increasing. While she didn't know what to do, she knew things had to change. It was time for her to look at her alternatives.

EXPLORE THE ALTERNATIVES

Kirstin needed to talk to someone who could help her figure out some options. She thought of her pastor but was afraid to go see him. Kirstin attended church so infrequently, she didn't think she had a right to seek his advice. That was not true. You don't have to earn the right to be safe. If there are people you trust, who might be able to help, don't hesitate to talk to them. Even if you don't know them very well, but understand them to be reliable sources of information, go ahead and seek their assistance.

Most states have domestic violence hotlines that provide referral resources. If you have no local source of information, give the hotline a try. If you can't find a listing for an agency dealing with domestic violence or a family crisis shelter, call your local mental health crisis clinic.

Don't forget to continue in prayer. It should be a high priority regardless of what else you do. Ask God for direction on what type of intervention to pursue (Matthew 21:22; John 17:7).

Following is a listing of services most frequently needed by families facing domestic violence. Seek out the phone numbers for these services; they will be helpful as you explore your alternatives.

- [ ] Abused women's support groups
- [ ] Alcohol drug treatment (residential and outpatient)
- [ ] Child Protective Services
- [ ] Child care (emergency, ongoing, and respite)
- [ ] Christian conciliation and mediation services (such as the Christian Legal Society)
- [ ] Court services (district, municipal, or superior)
- [ ] Counseling services
- [ ] Crisis center (24-hour availability on a telephone or walk-in basis)
- [ ] Emergency shelter for abused spouse and children
- [ ] Employment services (career counseling, job training, and placement)
- [ ] Family planning
- [ ] Financial assistance (such as Aid to Families with Dependent Children)
- [ ] Legal services
- [ ] Medical care (emergency and ongoing), family doctor
- [ ] Mental health services
- [ ] Permanent housing
- [ ] Police intervention
- [ ] Rape relief, sexual assault center
- [ ] Salvation Army (services and shelter)
- [ ] Shelters
- [ ] Transportation
- [ ] Victim Compensation Program
- [ ] Volunteer outreach
- [ ] YWCA resource center and/or shelter

If a moderate or high degree of risk is present for you or your children, the following alternatives need to be considered:

- ☐ Emergency shelter for you and your children
- ☐ Law enforcement involvement
- ☐ Court action
- ☐ Commitment of abuser to a mental health facility
- ☐ Placement of children in a safe environment
- ☐ Involvement of extended family, church, or community agencies in providing a place to stay and/or other necessities
- ☐ Medical assistance

Let's look at the possibilities for each of these alternatives: *Emergency or battered women's shelter.* A shelter is an important consideration because it deals with one of the most difficult problems for victims of domestic violence—where to go. Wife battering often takes place on weekends, late at night, or in the early-morning hours when everything is closed. Kirstin had packed up the kids one time after Tim had beaten her, but after driving around for an hour she discovered she had no place else to go. Her only option was to return home and encounter more torment.

Most shelters are located in their own homelike buildings whose addresses are not widely known. They can accommodate around twenty women and children in a safe and secure environment.

Shelters have a variety of philosophies undermining their operation. Some have a strong feminist orientation; others have a family perspective. If you are in a high-risk situation, worry about the philosophy later. Get to a safe place as soon as possible.

One advantage of a shelter over staying with family or friends is that it takes the pressure off of the family to keep your husband away from you. A shelter is used to dealing with angry husbands, and are fairly effective in keeping women and children safe while in the facility. Remember: *the shelter is only a temporary solution.* Usually a family can stay only about two weeks maximum. But it gives you a protected place to sort out your feelings and consider other options—and that is very important.

It can also be quite helpful to receive comfort and feedback from the other women in the shelter. And the staff at most shelters can provide some direction and resources for you, as you determine what to do next.

There *are* some disadvantages to going to a shelter. It is an abrupt change from the privacy of family living to a group-living situation. You will have to adapt to certain rules, such as sign-out procedures, curfews, and keeping the location confidential. A variety of social, ethnic, racial, and educational backgrounds will likely be represented, which can make adjustment more difficult for some. Usually the maintenance, cooking, and baby-sitting tasks must be shared by the residents.

Despite the problems of adjusting to a group environment, most find the experience to be positive. Follow-up studies have found that when the women decided to return to their mate, two-thirds of the time violence had not recurred. Furthermore, if violence did occur, it was less frequent and less severe than it had been before the women went to the shelters. About three-fourths of the women felt they had more control over their lives after their stay. The same number reported the batterer had taken steps to get counseling.[2]

These data give evidence of the positive effects of shelters. Divorce is by no means the most frequent decision made after staying in a shelter. Rather, it seems a majority of the time a shelter gives an abused woman some time and leverage to create change in a violent relationship. From this perspective, shelters can assist both you and your husband.

Law enforcement intervention. There are two reasons for discussing legal action. If you are in danger, legal intervention may help keep the abuser from imposing further injury or trauma. Second, legal intervention (court-ordered treatment) *may* be the *only* way to get your husband some help.

A law enforcement agency is usually called to intervene in a domestic disturbance because of its authority and twenty-four-hour availability. Besides, wife beating is a criminal offense in every state. But you need to know the limitations of law enforcement officers as well as their usefulness.

Many victims choose not to involve the police, yet police departments are still overwhelmed with family disturbance calls. Furthermore, the police seldom resolve the violence problem to everyone's satisfaction. Many localities classify assault-and-battery as a misdemeanor. This usually requires that the law enforcement officer be a witness to the assault before he can make an arrest. Often, the violence has ceased before the law enforcement officer arrives, and, of course, the abuser may deny any violence has occurred.

While it is sometimes difficult to obtain police intervention, evidence supports the fact that arresting the perpetrator of wife abuse generally achieves good results. The Minneapolis police department followed up on wife-beaters for six months to determine the effects of different police intervention. When the man was simply ordered out of the house, 22 percent repeated the offense. Of those who went through counseling, 16 percent repeated. But only 10 percent of those who were arrested beat their wives again.[3] In a West Coast study, the abuser was found to be 31 percent less likely to be reported again for violence if he was arrested.[4]

A general guideline would be not to call the police unless you mean business. Once you make the call, be prepared to follow through on signing a warrant or whatever other procedure is needed.

Keep in mind that police don't want to get involved in domestic violence. One out of five officers killed each year are fatally wounded while intervening in family disputes. Police are also limited in what they can do when they arrive at the scene. But if a high likelihood of danger exists, the police should definitely be called.

Sometimes the offender can be very drunk. If there is potential for injury, the officer may make the determination to take him to a detoxification unit rather than make an arrest.

The officer will advise you of the right to file an assault warrant, or other possible action, and may attempt to mediate a cooling-off time. Sometimes police are able to make referrals to community agencies and offer transportation to a safe place or to the station to file a warrant.

One more criterion must be considered when filing a police report. More states are establishing victim compensation programs for victims of domestic violence and other crimes. These programs can provide financial support for living, medical, and counseling expenses incurred as the victim. To get compensation, you or your representative must report the crime to law enforce-

151

ment officers within seventy-two hours, or as soon as reasonably possible. (Check the requirements in your area.) After that initial report, victims must apply within a specific period of time, usually one year, to the victim compensation program to obtain benefits. If you wait too long to report the incident, you may not be eligible for help.

If you are not willing to press assault charges against your husband, the police can do little, unless you live in one of the few states with mandatory arrest laws. They cannot make the man leave, because it's his home too.

Mandatory arrest laws. Domestic violence legislation in a few states has tried to deal with spouse abuse by giving police mandatory arrest authority in domestic disputes. Problems due to overzealous or inconsistent application of the law occasionally occur, but it is a major improvement.

Mandatory arrest laws give enforcement officers better guidelines for handling a complaint. If evidence exists of injury or the likelihood of injury, an officer is responsible to arrest the batterer. If the batterer has left the scene, police are obligated to search for a specified period of time, perhaps four hours.

Under the mandatory arrest law in Washington State, for example, if the batterer is arrested, he must post bail. He cannot be released on his personal recognizance. He must also sign a no-contact order which prohibits telephone, mail, third-party, or direct contact with the spouse.

Only four to six states have such legislation at the time of this writing, but the result is significantly more protection for the victim.

Court action—temporary restraining orders. Since only a few states have a mandatory arrest law, in the remaining states the chances of the police taking action are better if the woman has obtained a peace bond or a temporary restraining order. A peace bond requires the man to put up a certain amount of money, which he forfeits if he breaks his peace with the victim. Failure to post the bond can result in imprisonment. The peace bond may not be available in all states, so check with someone familiar with the law in your area.

A temporary restraining order is a legal document issued by a judge, and can be obtained without the man's presence. It requires the husband to stay away from the wife or to refrain from offensive conduct for a specific period of time. A restraining order is usually good for ten days, after which the man has the right to contest the order. A hearing could also be held at that time to determine if the order should be made permanent. If the restraining order is violated, the violator can be cited for contempt of court, which is a misdemeanor. Misdemeanor charges are generally resolved by fines, probation, or court-ordered counseling. Short jail sentences also are sometimes available.

Another problem is that, historically, a restraining order could be issued only after a divorce suit had been filed. If a woman was not willing to file for divorce, that form of protection was not available. Recent domestic violence laws have been altered in some states so that a dissolution procedure does not have to be initiated in order to issue a temporary restraining order.

Other states operate under a different process called a temporary protection order, or order of protection. This order is in effect for up to fourteen days and does not require divorce action. At the end of the period, a hearing is held to determine if a permanent order should be granted.

Because each state is different, check with a domestic violence hotline or other resource to become aware of the procedures available in your region.

It may seem unduly harsh to consider taking legal action against your husband. Consider, please, two ideas. First, has doing it your way worked? Have your attempts to love, demand, plead, or manipulate brought about corrective changes? Second, most violent men need an authority figure, definite structure, and punitive consequences to direct them to change their behavior. Taking steps to obtain a court order, for example, may not seem so harsh when it stops the abuse and leads to long-term help.

Commitment of abuser to mental health facility. Unless your husband is willing to enter a hospital, this option has limited possibilities. The involuntary commitment laws vary from state to state, but do have some commonalities. The process begins when any concerned person initiates a call to the involuntary commitment team or the police. If the mental health unit is called, a "flying squadron" of mental health professionals may come to see the person in question. Their purpose is to make a determination of whether the abuser could be committed against his will. If the batterer is totally out of control, the police may be involved and can take him to a mental health facility where the evaluation is done.

The determination to commit an individual is based on whether he is judged to be of high danger to himself or others. The criteria is pretty stringent, and almost requires the person to have a gun to his head or pointed at his wife.

If the team believes the person is at risk to himself or others, he will be immediately taken to a mental health facility for a period of observation not exceeding seventy-two hours. At the end of that time, one of three things can happen: (1) the person can be judged no longer a risk and released; (2) the abuser may voluntarily agree to enter a treatment program; or (3) a petition can be filed to commit the person for up to fourteen days. If the person still meets the criteria for commitment after the two-week period, the formal legal process continues, possibly involving a jury trial, which can result in commitment for three to six months.

Most involuntary commitments are terminated after the initial seventy-two-hour period because most people cannot be shown, at that moment, to be dangerous to themselves or others. At any point, they can *voluntarily* keep themselves in treatment, but it is difficult to maintain the criteria for *involuntary* retention.

Placement of children in a safer environment. Many victims of wife battering will tolerate a great deal of pain—until it begins to affect their children. The caution here is that your children have already been affected.

In the first place, they may have been victimized as much as you. They may have been exposed to direct physical abuse when, during the course of the parents' fighting, the violence shifted directly to the children. Usually this is done in the name of discipline. A child starts crying because the parents are fighting, and the abusive parent slaps the child to get her to stop.

Some children have been hurt accidentally during out-of-control family arguments; for example, the mother drops the baby while avoiding the abuser. Others have been injured when a frustrated father projects blame onto the child for the problems of the family. Children also have been mistreated when the problems in the marriage shift to disappointments in the child—for example, harsh punishment because the child brings home a poor report card.

Children have been abused when the mother takes out her frustrations and aggressions on the child since she can't retaliate toward her husband. Finally, the child may become a direct target for the abuser's violence, along with the wife. This may be particularly true when the father resents the child in some way or when he or she is a stepchild.

Emotional abuse can also impact a child in a violence prone family. For example, many children take the blame for their parents' fights, and spend years dealing with false guilt for the plight of the family. If the parents are caught up in marriage problems, the child's needs for praise, encouragement, and quality time may be ignored. Children may be left to fix meals for themselves, or have to get themselves off to school, because Mom is in bed with injuries and Dad has stormed out of the house.

These are the direct forms of abuse that can affect a child. The second major consideration, less observable short-term, but crucial over a lifetime, is the well-documented fact that children raised in abusive families have a much higher chance of being abusers themselves. If you can't manage to take action for your own welfare, think about the future of your children. Do you want them victimized any further or perhaps grow up to abuse their families?

If these considerations strike a responsive chord, then, in addition to the previous options, you may consider having your children live elsewhere for a time. Could they stay with extended family—grandparents, aunts and uncles, older siblings? What about temporary arrangements such as summer camp, working for a friend or relative, or foster care?

It is better if the child can stay with his or her family, because to remove the child is to risk him or her taking more blame for the family problems. Removal, however, may still be the safer alternative. Needless to say, the decision is a hard one, and it should only be considered along with the question of what are you going to do to stop the abuse in the children's absence.

Involvement of extended family or community. Let's return to Kirstin's story:

> Kirstin knew she had to do something. While going through her list of options, she suddenly remembered her aunt who lived in Portland. Kirstin had stayed with Aunt Brenda for a

couple of weeks one summer in high school. They had become very close, and she had told Kirstin to give her a call if she ever needed any help. While she hadn't talked to her aunt for some time, Kirstin knew her relative had meant her promise.

School would be starting in a few weeks, so if they did go to Portland they would need to do something right away. It was difficult to think about leaving, but as Kirstin considered her options, calling Aunt Brenda seemed like the best thing to do.

If you consider asking family or friends to provide housing, they should be assured it is a temporary commitment. Try to check out sources of financial support before you contact them, so they can be assured you won't be a financial drain. In some cases, you may have no choice but to borrow money. Try to be a good steward, but don't avoid taking action for your own safety and long-term welfare.

Also remind them it is illegal for your abusive husband to enter their residence without their permission, and that they can call the police, if necessary, to remove him from their property. Legal action, described earlier, may also be needed to ensure your safety.

Don't let embarrassment or isolation keep you from checking out resources in your church. There may be several families who would be glad to help. The church is a place for hurting people. Right now you hurt. Draw on those resources. Check with your pastor, elder, or deacon. It is a risk, but they may be able to help better than anyone else you know.

Medical attention. Victims of family violence are often fearful of using medical services. Don't omit this important consideration. First, your own health is critical. Some kinds of injuries, left untreated, can bring a lifetime of discomfort. Internal injuries can become life-threatening. Injuries can also lower your general resistance to other diseases. Again, don't neglect your physical welfare!

Second, it is important to obtain medical evidence of your abuse. You will need a doctor's report and other proof to back up any charges you may make against the abuser. The same evidence would also be needed in applying for victim compensation.

DEVELOP AND IMPLEMENT YOUR PLAN

As you consider these alternatives, and perhaps talk them over with someone, eventually a plan will emerge. No one can tell you how to make a decision. You alone must examine your options, buckle up your courage, and take action.

No one deserves to be beaten or threatened. There are no excuses for abusive behavior. Violence at home will not just go away. But if you take action and reach out for help, it can be stopped.

* * * * *

This chapter has given you a chance to look at alternatives to ensure your safety and to bring the abusive situation to a point where change can occur. This is the crisis phase—very uncomfortable but necessary. The next chapter will examine the kind of emotional changes needed by both the victim and the abuser to bring the marriage back to health.

NOTES

1. Adapted from William A. Stacey and Anson Shupe, *The Family Secret: Domestic Violence in America* (Boston: Beacon Press), 1983, pp. 122-127. Used by permission.
2. Stacey and Shupe, *The Family Secret*, pp. 150-151.
3. Susan Jacoby, *The New York Times*, May 5, 1983.
4. Vincent Bozzi, "Arrest Deters Batterers," in *Psychology Today*, August, 1986, p. 8.

CHAPTER ELEVEN

Changing the Cycle

Overcoming the Problems of Spouse Abuse

After considering all her options, Kirstin decided to go stay with her aunt. She had to do something to stop the beatings. Her husband, Tim, was furious at first. He finally traced where she had gone and caused such a scene the police had to be called. Reluctantly, Kirstin obtained an order of protection. Tim maintained he had a right to see the children no matter what a judge said. The next time he came to the house demanding to visit Tommy and Cammie, Kirstin called the police again and Tim ended up in jail.

The outcome of Tim's defying the court order was positive. The judge ordered Tim to get counseling or face a term in jail. So, with much reluctance, Tim entered a group for men who batter, sponsored by a Christian counseling service.

If she had it to do over again, Kirstin would have taken action to have Tim move out of the home instead of her and the children. But at the time, she was so afraid she couldn't think of anything else. After a couple of months, Kirstin decided to return home.

By the time Kirstin and the children returned, Tim was beginning to admit his problems and seemed to be making sincere efforts to understand himself. The court requirement for counseling was still in effect, so Kirstin felt comfortable Tim would continue treatment. She probably wouldn't have come home otherwise.

The separation also taught Kirstin some things about herself. She had found a part-time job and received good feedback from her boss. She really didn't want to work while the children were young, but she found she could do it if she had to. Kirstin also started counseling sessions with her pastor and began to see some of the ways she had fed into the cycle of abuse.

Tim and Kirstin still had a lot to learn, but the battering had stopped. The first priority—safety—had been reached. Now they could begin to build a healthier way of responding to one another.

It took a great deal of courage, along with a combination of legal and social services, but Kirstin had helped bring a stop to her abuse. She no longer lived in constant fear of violence in her own home. Her first goal had been met. Now she and Tim could work on some of the behavior patterns that caused the battering in the first place.

How to change the cycle of abuse is the focus of this chapter. Many topics in the area of personal and marriage enrichment could be covered. Space allows only a discussion of those topics particularly unique to spouse abuse. As a point of departure, let's look at those issues relevant to the wife.

ISSUES FOR THE BATTERED WOMAN

Continued safety. After she moved back home, one of the first things Kirstin's pastor covered in their counseling sessions was an escape plan. You also should have such a plan. The plan should be specific and detailed, including alternatives for transportation, a place to stay, who to call for help, financial arrangements, and plans for work or school. Your husband should not know the specifics of the plan. You want to hope for the best, but relapses do occur. The first ground rule for reconciliation is no violence under any circumstances. If that rule is broken, you need to have a definite response in mind. If you don't, you risk getting into old habits of helplessness. This must not happen.

All too frequently wives allow themselves to be reunited with their abusive husbands before they have had a chance to change. This increases the chances that the cycle of violence will be repeated. Only after the husband has made significant progress in controlling his violence should a focus on marriage counseling begin.

What if your husband won't change? In our example, Tim eventually decided to acknowledge his lack of self-control and made efforts to change. This gave Kirstin hope and opportunity to work on restoration of the marriage. This is the most positive outcome in a violence-prone family. But what if your husband denies his problem with abuse?

In such a situation you have several options: return to the marriage with no guarantee of changes; leave the marriage— either by separation or divorce; return to the marriage on the promise your husband will change; or return only after seeing evidence your husband has changed.

Making decisions is difficult for many abused wives, due to such factors as fear, financial dependency, and a commitment to the marriage. You do have the responsibility, however, and you must take appropriate action. Consider the following response from Dr. James Dobson to a woman who had been abused over the twelve years of her marriage. Her violent husband was a leader in their church and a prominent attorney.

> In essence, Laura is being emotionally blackmailed by her husband. He is saying by his behavior, "Do what I wish or I'll beat you." She must break out of that tyranny while she's still young enough to cope with the consequences. This might be accomplished by forcing the matter to a crisis. . . . I would suggest that Laura choose the most absurd demand her husband makes, and then refuse to consent to it. Let him rage if he must rage. . . . Separate living quarters may be necessary until her husband settles down. He should be made to *think* that he has lost his wife over this issue, and in fact, I would recommend that she not return until there is reason to believe that he is willing to change. If that takes a

year, so be it. When (and if) her husband acknowledges that he has a severe problem and promises to deal with it if she'll come home, a period of negotiations should follow.... I don't believe anyone should be required to live in that kind of terror, and in fact, to do so is to tolerate a behavior which could eventually prove fatal to the marriage, anyway.'

This "love must be tough" response is difficult and risky, but the options are even more disastrous.

Low self-esteem. One of the primary goals for a battered wife is to learn to love herself in spite of her abusive history. Self-esteem develops from many sources. To know the home is safe, not living in dread and terror of the next violent incident, is a beginning.

Another ingredient is having the freedom to learn new tasks. When the husband learns to allow his wife to take classes, sing in the choir, volunteer at the community center, or even to get her driver's license, her confidence will grow. You gain self-esteem as you learn to be competent in areas that have meaning to you. Take some positive risks. This kind of risk-taking can be fun!

Another related component of self-esteem is to have an accurate vision of your personal possibilities. God has made you whole and complete (2 Corinthians 5:17; Colossians 3:10). If you can understand and accept yourself, you will be able to grow toward that essential completeness.

Acknowledge the existence of your personality defects, social inadequacies, or spiritual failures. As a battered wife, you have endured injustice and made some poor decisions. Admitting these problem areas is not incompatible with growth. In fact, it is necessary.

Your growth toward a better self-image doesn't stop with the recognition of weakness and inadequacies, however. The process must move on to an appropriate love of yourself.

The reason failure and trauma can be stepping-stones to improved self-esteem resides in the fact of God's unconditional love for us (John 3:16; 16:27). You are loved regardless of your personal failures. You have done nothing to deserve God's love, yet it is freely given (Romans 5:15-17).

The statement to "love our neighbor" is repeated several times in Scripture, but never without the command to love yourself

(Romans 13:9; Galatians 5:14; James 2:8). God knows it's important to love ourselves, even though we don't naturally do a very good job of it.

Some of the facts of God's love were summarized in chapter 8. Look again at those realities of God's love for you.

Another stepping-stone in developing a complete self-image is the issue of your purpose for living—"Why am I here?" Knowing why God placed you on earth will give you a compass bearing, enabling you to cooperate with His intention. In other words, it gives your life a sense of direction.

Our calling is to be God's representatives on earth. As stewards of all that He created, we have the major purpose of bearing fruit. "You did not choose Me, but I chose you to go and bear fruit— fruit that will last. Then the Father will give you whatever you ask in My name" (John 15:16).

This Scripture and others (Matthew 3:8; Romans 7:4; Philippians 1:11; Colossians 1:10) encourage us to use our abilities and our gifts in service for others. Then the fruits of love, joy, peace, patience, kindness, goodness, faithfulness, gentleness, and self-control will be planted, nourished, and multiplied (Galatians 5:22-23).

Despite an abusive history, you can find hope in your reason for existence. By focusing on the nature of your fruit and how to increase your productivity, you will make a major contribution to your self-esteem and self-confidence.

The last ingredient of self-esteem is your relationship to the rest of the Christian community. The battered woman has experienced significant isolation. This component speaks to that feeling of separation and abandonment.

This relationship to the rest of the body of believers is possible because we are all called to be ministers of God (Isaiah 61:6; 2 Corinthians 6:4). Each Christian is part of the priesthood of believers (Exodus 19:6; 1 Peter 2:5). This means there are no positions of a "higher calling." We are all called to glorify God and to serve. As believers, we are all equally accountable for how well our responsibilities are carried out.

Each of us has been given different talents and abilities. We are exposed to different opportunities. The common task is to put to wise use what we've been given. You are a part of that opportunity. Take it slow. You're probably not used to sharing your talents and gifts. But you do have them, and the rest of the fellowship needs your contribution.

Resentment and anger. Your abuse has probably contributed to feelings of anger, along with bitterness and resentment. Reread the section on anger in chapter 8. Your husband's violence must stop, but you are accountable for what you do with your feelings of retaliation and revenge.

Changing unrealistic hope. You want your marriage to succeed. You probably still have sincere love and loyalty to your husband, in spite of the pain you have endured. The task now is to move from unrealistic to realistic expectations for your marriage.

You saw earlier how a bonding can develop during the remorse phase of the violent cycle. When things seemed better for a little while, and your husband promised to change, you tended to cling to those hopes and dreams. But inevitably the tension would build toward another episode of abuse.

Your goal here is to avoid the trap of appeasement. You must get rid of the idea that you can keep your husband from getting angry. You cannot control his feelings or make decisions for him on how he will handle those feelings. Learn to back off.

In the past, when you saw a potential source of frustration, you have stepped in to smooth things out. Kirstin, for example, would give in to her children's request for treats or special privileges more readily when she knew Tim was in a bad mood. This was bad for the children, but kept the distractions to a minimum. Later, Kirstin found it was legitimate for her to respond to the children in terms of what was best for them. If they cried a little while because they didn't get their way, so be it. This was one of life's little frustrations that Tim had to learn to handle.

It's like a flock of servants preceding the king down a city street. They scurry about sweeping away all the pebbles and laying down the red carpet for His Majesty. It would be most horrible if His Magnificence was to step on a stone! Such a shame. Meanwhile his feet remain soft and pampered because they have never had to deal with the realities of life.

Let your husband learn to walk on his own two feet.

Eliminating isolation. You need social contact. Try to reestablish family and social connections. Reach out to your extended family. Your husband may be more receptive to social gatherings if you're not healing from bruises. Have some fun. Join a bowling team. Play volleyball at the Y. Exercise is good for the body and gives you a chance to make friends.

You may also want to join an abused women's support group. Your counselor, pastor, or domestic violence resource center can probably help you find such a group.

Expand your knowledge of community resources. This was discussed earlier, but it will continue to be important. Know the phone numbers and descriptions of the various social and community services. See chapter 10 for examples of the resources you might need.

Finally, remember that the Apostle Paul experienced stoning, beating, flogging, shipwrecks, and imprisonment, yet his God did not leave him. Think of the following statement whenever you feel abandoned: "For I am convinced that neither death nor life, neither angels nor demons, neither the present nor the future, nor any powers, neither height nor depth, nor anything else in all creation, will be able to separate us from the love of God that is in Christ Jesus our Lord" (Romans 8:38-39).

Overcoming emotional dependency and learned helplessness. The term *learned helplessness* has been used to explain why women have found it difficult to escape an abusive relationship. This is how it works.

If you take a laboratory animal, place it in a cage, and then proceed to administer electric shock to the cage floor at random intervals, a curious thing will happen. When the animal is exposed to the painful situation long enough, and if there is no way of escape, he will give up. You can turn off the shock machine, open the cage door, and the animal will cower in a corner, making no effort to escape. His motivation to scramble for freedom has been traumatized away.

As a battered woman you have had the same kind of experience. Your attempts to control the violence have not worked, so your motivation to do something different is reduced to zero.

Now you must learn new methods of survival. You need to learn how to activate and channel healthy anger, rather than becoming depressed or blaming yourself. Now that you have taken action to stop the abuse, you must also believe you can do something to make a difference in your life. The door of the cage is open. Take advantage of the opportunity.

God doesn't transform you by eliminating all your problems;

He changes you by renewing your mind. By letting your mind dwell only on those things that are true, honorable, pure, and lovely, you will win the battle over worry and anxiety, as well as over feelings of helplessness (Philippians 4:6-9).[2]

Traditional view of marriage.[3] There is nothing wrong with the "traditional" marriage, but there is a great deal wrong with a husband who uses violence to maintain his position within the marriage. Neither is it wrong for you to be committed to the sanctity and permanence of marriage. The problem of many battered wives is that they haven't been able to separate commitment from unhealthy tolerance.

One of the major issues for the Christian wife is the principle of submission. Many a battered wife has gone for help only to be told she should be more submissive. The concepts of submission and headship are clearly biblical. The confusion comes because of the multitude of explanations as to their meanings.

Many women have been told the secret to a happy marriage is for the wife to accept a dependent role to her husband. She is to adapt to him rather than expect him to change. But if the husband is abusive, the wife is put into a box. If she puts up with his violence, she is the victim of pain. If she takes action to stop his violence, she feels guilty for being outside the chain of command.

That's where the equally biblical idea of *mutual subjection* comes in. In Ephesians 5:21-33, Paul begins with the explicit statement, "Submit to one another out of reverence for Christ." Paul realizes relationships in a family are meant to be reciprocal and accountable. There must be equal give and take in a family for growth to occur. No happiness is found when one member dominates, without respect for the needs and feelings of the rest of the family.

Submission also includes accountability. Accountability means being responsible for what you say or do. A husband asks his wife to hold him accountable, and she asks the same of him. It is love in action as the wife helps her husband grow toward wholeness by asking him to demonstrate responsibility. It should work both ways.

Abusive relationships are not reciprocal, unless that means fighting fire with fire. Healthy motivation is found through mutual adaptation. The wife is not the only one who needs to adapt. The husband must sometimes do what his wife needs, even if it conflicts with some of his own desires.

The goal of marriage is oneness (Genesis 2:24). With this goal in mind, Paul gave instructions to each marriage partner. To husbands, he said, "Love your wives, just as Christ loved the church and gave Himself up for her" (Ephesians 5:25). And to the wives he said, "Submit to your husbands as to Christ the Lord" (Ephesians 5:22). Your goal is to develop a mutual relationship, in which each of you attempts to love Christ and have a servant's heart.

The topics of headship and submission will be developed a bit more later in this chapter.

ISSUES FOR THE ABUSIVE HUSBAND

Tim entered the counseling office with an obvious chip on his shoulder. He was still angry about Kirstin leaving him. But that wasn't the whole story. When he found out where she was staying and went there to see the kids, he ended up in jail. He hadn't been in jail since that little altercation in high school. True, he did beat up several other guys after a football game. But they had it coming.

Anyway, this was different. He had a right to see his kids. The fact that he had taken a sledgehammer to the front door wasn't that big of a deal.

But the judge had said, "Take a six-month anger management class, or spend six months in jail."

It wasn't much of a choice. So, here he was. As Tim slumped down into a chair in the corner of the room, he surveyed the rest of the "wife beaters" out of the corner of his eye.

"They all look like a bunch of jerks to me," he thought. "I wonder if they all got tossed out by their wives too? Boy, I'm still so mad about this whole thing I could punch my fist through that wall right now!"

Before Tim could continue his daydream any further, the male and female counselors entered the room, and the first session began.

Men who batter their wives are also victims. They are casualties of their uncontrolled anger, their inability to express feelings, a fear of closeness, and their dependency on the women they batter. Inside each man who abuses is a scared little boy who desperately needs warmth and security. Unfortunately, his way of showing his fear terrorizes others.

Entire books are devoted to treatment of men who batter. This discussion will include only a few relevant topics that apply to the Christian reader. It will parallel most of the characteristics of abusers presented earlier.

General principles for growth. Abusive anger is a learned behavior that comes out of the basic nature of humankind. All humanity is inclined to oppose God's best wishes for health and maturity. It is a constant fact of history that man tends to inflict pain on others. Since this happens on a societal level, it comes as no surprise that it occurs at a family level.

Because we assume violence is learned, it is equally possible to replace the abusive behavior with new and appropriate actions. This process works much better if the man accepts God's work of grace into his life. If he doesn't, his growth is limited to his human understanding and finite resources.

The abuser is solely responsible for his own violent actions. Excuses cannot be accepted. No matter how many stressors there are, violence is not justified in marriage. Choice is always involved in violence and each person must be held accountable for that choice. A victim cannot cause or eliminate the violent action of the abuser. Sure, an argument can be irritating. Sure, someone can rub you the wrong way. But another person cannot *make* you use violence.

Sources of help. Changes usually don't take place without outside help. Group counseling seems to be the most effective treatment for men who batter. The group is able to help break through the denial and minimizing so common among abusers. The group helps each member realize that other men have similar problems. Experience in a group also helps men who batter overcome some of their emotional isolation from other men. It helps those who lack interpersonal skills enhance their ability to relate to others.

After group members get to know each other, they will often reach out to each other in times of crisis, which can be a very helpful lesson in learning how to give and receive comfort or assistance. Most men don't know how to do this very well.

Some programs are designed around a self-help group approach modeled after Alcoholics Anonymous. Called Batterers Anonymous, this can be a vital part of the treatment process.

Individual counseling and marriage counseling are also important components of a treatment program. Marriage counseling should only be started after the husband has made significant progress in controlling his anger. Marriage counseling will not work if the wife still lives in dread of the next outburst.

Anger control. Man is not disturbed by events, but by the view he takes of them. Anger control for the abusive husband is developed by teaching how beliefs, values, and thoughts create anger. Outward action, such as aggression, is a product of internal thoughts. "For as [a man] thinketh in his heart, so is he" (Proverbs 23:7, KJV).

Anger results from how a person perceives his situation and what he tells himself about the consequences of that situation. For example, "She didn't iron my shirt last night. I need that shirt. She should have known I would need it. She doesn't care about my needs. I must have my needs met all of the time. Therefore, I must show her my displeasure so it won't happen again."

All this may take place instantly inside the mind. It is this silent monologue that builds within the abuser, and eventually results in aggression. This is particularly true when he doesn't know how else to handle a problem. Most abusers do not have the ability to resolve conflict through conversation, compromise, or other problem-solving techniques. Most batterers have only two ways to handle their anger—hold it in (at least for a while), or express it in a hostile form. Either way, the outcome doesn't work very well. This sense of powerlessness produces more frustration, which in turn makes violence more likely. The resulting lowered self-esteem leads to feelings of depression. This adds to the frustration, and it becomes an endless cycle.

The goal of treatment is to teach men (and women) how to avoid anger in the first place, and how to express anger in non-violent ways. The initial step in many programs is to teach the abuser how to be aware of the build-up of his feelings. A frequent comment made by men who batter is, "All of a sudden I find myself in a blind rage, and I'm out of control. I couldn't help myself." They seldom connect a sequence of events or thoughts to the eventual act of violence. A journal, anger log, or diary is often used to develop this awareness.

Additional points of focus are: ground rules for handling anger, such as a time out; the effects of self-talk on feelings; and dealing with irrational beliefs that underlie most aggressive behaviors. Abusive men have a choice in how they think. The type of thoughts you choose influences how you will feel. This knowledge will eventually produce more self-control.

Jealousy. "For jealousy arouses a husband's fury, and he will show no mercy when he takes revenge" (Proverbs 6:34). Jealous episodes are among the most common precipitants of family violence. Jealousy is tied to the degree of insecurity the husband has about the relationship. The more insecure he is, the more jealous he will be.

Power is also an important ingredient in jealousy. Marriage is usually most satisfying when an even distribution of power exists—when neither spouse's desires automatically prevail. The concept of mutual submission seems relevant here. If the couple can learn to share and compromise, they will be doing a lot to inoculate themselves against harmful jealousy.

Self-esteem and assertiveness. If the other aspects of the treatment program are working, the abuser should be gaining some measure of satisfaction and pride. This sense of increasing success and competency will certainly improve his self-esteem.

The discussion earlier in this chapter of self-esteem from God's point of view is as appropriate for the abuser as for the victim.

Assertive action involves awareness of your own needs as well as the needs of others. Assertiveness includes being honest and direct with your feelings and desires. It may involve persistence when someone else does not agree. An assertive person respects the rights of someone else to deny his requests. Being able to pose compromises is an important assertive skill. It also involves confident body language: posture, gestures, and voice. Assertiveness usually results in feeling good about yourself because it does a better job of meeting your needs. That results in more self-confidence, which in turn causes others to respond more positively.

Rigid application of traditional sex roles.[4] For the Christian, the "traditional" roles in marriage are still perfectly valid and functional. The problem is the inflexible and demanding position taken by most men who batter. For the aggressive husband, a direct relationship often exists between his level of insecurity and the intensity with which he demands authority in the home. If the husband makes a major issue out of headship, submission, and obedience, he probably has questions about himself. A man with a poor self-image is going to look for affirmation by exerting power over his family, and he may even use Scripture as a source of authority. But his primary motivation comes from his own insecurity. The more intense his demands, the greater his insecurity.

Desiring a place of power and authority is a risky business. Internal conflict is likely because the man believes he must maintain his status as head of the household despite his weaknesses. For the abusive male, this creates resentment, which leads to more violence to regain his dominant position.

A basic question at this point is whether the husband *should* always have to be dominant. For the Christian man, the primary source of his *should* is found in the teachings about headship and submission.

Ephesians 5 brings the concepts of headship and submission together. The idea of mutual submission is the basis for Paul's presentation (v. 21), and its application was discussed earlier in the section on helping battered women. Now we will look at the rest of Paul's argument.

Based on mutual submission, Paul expands on the meaning of headship, moving the idea toward the oneness which God initially intended for marriage (Genesis 2:24). The emphasis on headship is no longer to be rank or power, but *self-giving servanthood.*

Paul uses the example of Christ's self-sacrificing action on behalf of the church not to say that the husband should become a lord and master, like Christ. The purpose of the comparison is to show headship becoming a means of responsibility and initiative—responsibility to act in love and initiative to act in service. As Christ gave Himself in love and humbled Himself, so husbands are to take the initiative in building an atmosphere of loving, self-sacrificing service in their marriage and home.

The idea of the body of Christ, the church, being composed of many parts, each fulfilling a unique purpose, seems to apply in this context. Because individuals in any family have widely varying skills and abilities, it may be that at different times particular persons will provide the leadership which moves the group forward. Headship in marriage is seen as accepting the responsibility and performing certain functions so that the relationship is advanced toward the goal of oneness.

Of course, the members of the body of Christ are individually responsible and accountable to God for their own actions. Nothing in Ephesians 5 suggests that either partner is more responsible for achieving Creation's goal of oneness. A different function is given to each person, but two independent, equal people are to become one.

The husband's headship should move him to become a servant to his wife in the same way as Christ is a servant to His church. Just as Christ creates conditions whereby the church may become whole and clean, so the husband is to create opportunities for his wife to move toward maturity and fulfillment as a person. Within the context of servanthood, a wife is to submit to her husband. This subjection must allow her to retain her respect for her husband, since the subjection is to be of similar quality and nature as the church being subject to Christ. Several points seem important from Paul's discussion.

First, the woman is subject to her husband, not to all men. There would seem to be no justification in interpreting this passage to suggest that women must always act through the opinions of any man simply because of their sex.

Second, the woman is to be active, responsible, and involved in a positive and creative way. Though the church is to be subject to Christ, we find a great deal of freedom and initiative given into the hands of the church. The church is to use every resource and gift at its disposal to maintain a relationship with God and to fulfill the Great Commission, fully active and energetic in its outreach. The wife is also to be active, not passive.

Third, the wife is to be honest and genuine in her relationship to her husband. She is not to use any ploys or forms of manipulation to get her husband to fulfill her selfish wishes. Submission is not a sophisticated form of manipulation.

Fourth, the wife is not under responsibility to obey her husband if he asks her to commit immoral or illegal acts. The example of Sapphira in Acts 5 demonstrates this. She was brought before Peter and quizzed as to whether she had agreed to her husband's deception. She was judged by her own action, and not because she was carrying out her husband's wishes.

Fifth, the wife is commanded to respect her husband. You can only respect someone else if your own self-image is positive. Behaving exclusively at the command of the husband does not allow a woman to maintain her self-dignity. Respect can come only when he acts in fairness and competency. The husband is to cultivate his wife's gifts and personality, not demand allegiance. You cannot demand respect. This is another area where the action of an abusive husband is counterproductive. Submission does not include blotting out the wife's personality or feelings. To do so denies the gifts God has given her to be used to foster and nurture the marriage relationship.

In the final analysis, acting out mutual subjection, headship, and submission within a given marriage is an open and creative matter. No single mold is to be used to determine how each couple should act. Headship means that both husband and wife live under the headship of Christ, submitting to Him and discovering His guidance for their marriage.

The key principle here is *choice.* Given a variety of options for growth, a couple has more freedom to grow. To be submissive means to yield in humble and intelligent obedience to a power or authority that God has ordained. This is to be done out of freedom and love, not out of compulsion and fear. Both husband and wife are free to choose the pattern that best fits them, just as we are free to choose Christ. Then, if a wife does not submit to her husband in the way that God intends, or when the husband does not demonstrate servanthood love to his wife, a spiritual as well as a marital problem may exist.

NOTES

1. James C. Dobson, *Love Must Be Tough* (Waco, Texas: Word), 1983, pp. 148-149.
2. Grant L. Martin, *Transformed By Thorns* (Wheaton, Ill.: Victor Books), 1985, pp. 95-115.
3. Adapted from Grant L. Martin, *Counseling for Family Violence and Abuse* (Waco, Texas: Word), 1987, pp. 88-91.
4. Ibid., pp. 117-121.

CHAPTER TWELVE

Pains of the Aged

The Nature and Scope of Elder Abuse

Grandma Miller was seventy-five last month. She lived with her son and daughter-in-law. It wasn't the best of arrangements, but after her husband died several years ago, Grandma couldn't afford to stay in the same retirement center. Her son, Ben, was having financial problems of his own, and Sarah was expecting their third child. At the time, everybody thought it was a mutual advantage to have Grandma stay with Ben's family. Her pension money would help make the house payments, and she liked the idea of being with the grandchildren.

In the past two years Grandma's health has deteriorated rapidly. She has taken much more care than Sarah expected. This, along with the two-year-old, and Ben having to work overtime to make ends meet, put Sarah under extreme pressure.

Sarah loved Grandma, but she found herself resenting the time and energy it took to care for her. Grandma took to spending more and more time in her room, and that was just fine with Sarah. Sometimes Sarah neglected to give

Grandma her medicine, so she would double the dose the next time. If Grandma ever commented or complained about her situation, Sarah would tell her to "shut up," and refuse to take in the next meal. Pretty soon Grandma quit saying anything.

Grandma had to ask Ben several times for her bank records. When she finally got them, she noticed her savings account was almost depleted. Ben denied knowing anything was unusual. He told her, "You're just getting too senile to remember anything. You haven't had much money in there since we paid your hospital bill last year."

Grandma knew that wasn't true. She had seen the receipts. She didn't know what to believe. Maybe she *was* getting too senile to remember. Sometimes she wished she could die.

It was difficult deciding how to write this chapter. Unlike spouse abuse, this chapter is not likely to be read by the victims, since most are quite aged and have multiple illnesses. In this respect, my objectives are similar to those found in dealing with the topic of child abuse. I am probably writing to either a concerned caretaker, such as a nurse, or to a non-offending relative. Some readers will be interested individuals such as pastors and family friends. A few of you may even be perpetrators of the abuse, perhaps unintentionally.

The primary goal of this chapter is to heighten your awareness of the problem. The 1960s was the decade of awareness for child abuse. In the 1970s, domestic violence was focused on spouse abuse. And elder abuse appears to be the dominant theme of the 1980s. Some research has been done, but relatively little is known about abuse of the elderly, compared to child and spouse abuse. If you finish this chapter with an increased sensitivity to the plight of the elderly and a renewed commitment to do what you can to help an elderly person in your field of influence, my objectives will have been met.

INCIDENCE OF ELDER ABUSE
According to the U.S. Census Bureau, in 1980 about 25½ million Americans were age sixty-five or older. People are living longer.

The life expectancy in the United States has risen to seventy-four years in this century. In 1900, one of eleven Americans was sixty-five or older. Today the statistic is one in nine, which accounts for about 11 percent of the total population.

It is projected that by the year 2000, about one in five citizens will be sixty-five or older. This translates to about 31 million older adults by that time, and 45 million by 2020.[1] Our society is rapidly becoming one characterized by aged children caring for frail, elderly parents. Unfortunately, things are not going very well for the elderly.

The House Select Committee on Aging submitted a report for the Congressional Record in May, 1985. The Committee concluded that about 4 percent of the nation's elderly may be victims of some sort of abuse—from moderate to severe. In fact, about 1.1 million older Americans may be victims of abuse every year, which would include one out of every twenty-five Americans.[2]

While these figures are high, they may only be a fraction of the total problem. The Committee on Aging reported that while one out of three child abuse cases is reported, only one out of six cases of adult abuse ever comes to the attention of authorities.

The average person may find it hard to believe how widespread the problem really seems to be. It cuts across all classes of society. Abuse of the elderly occurs in small towns, large cities, suburbs, and in rural areas.

Here are some examples of abuse included in the report by the Committee on Aging:

> A seventy-eight-year-old New York woman in a wheelchair was repeatedly assaulted by her thirty-six-year-old grandson. As a result of twelve assaults, she was hospitalized seven times for injuries as severe as hip fractures. When police responded to assault reports, the woman refused to testify against her grandson and did not want him arrested. However, witnesses were secured and the grandson was jailed on counts of assault and robbery of his grandmother. Released on bail, pending trial, he returned home and beat her again. He was then convicted and sentenced to three to seven years in prison.

* * * * *

In South Carolina, a sixty-eight-year-old woman living with her daughter was found by a caseworker in conditions of unspeakable squalor. The woman was kept in an unheated portion of the house where the temperature was less than 20 degrees. When found, the woman had eight soiled blankets piled over her head to keep her warm and the urine from her catheter was frozen. She was also malnourished. She developed pneumonia and was hospitalized. Upon discharge, authorities had her placed in a nursing home.

* * * * *

An arthritic, slightly obese, but otherwise healthy Iowa woman lived with her daughter and twenty-two-year-old grandson who reportedly physically and sexually abused her. The daughter admitted there was familial conflict and wanted her mother to move. The mother was turning over $300 of her $320 monthly Social Security check to the daughter.[3]

America may be the most powerful and advanced civilization in the world, yet thousands of elderly Americans are victims of chronic, continuing patterns of emotional and physical abuse and neglect. Until we can live up to the commandment to honor our fathers and mothers, we cannot make any real claims to being "advanced" in any moral or ethical sense.

TYPES OF ELDER ABUSE
The most commonly accepted categories and definitions of abuse include:

Physical abuse. This includes willful infliction of physical pain, malnutrition, mental anguish, or injuries such as bruises, welts, sprains, dislocations, abrasions, or lacerations. The use of disciplinary restraints, such as straps, chains, or locked rooms, are considered physical abuse. Willful deprivation of services necessary to maintain physical or mental health, such as meals, clothing, or adequate shelter, constitute other examples of physical abuse. Also included are sexual abuse, restrictions on freedom of movement, unreasonable confinement, and murder.

Psychological abuse. Verbal assaults, threats, taunting, condemnation, provocation of fear, and isolation—either physical or emotional, can leave deep emotional scars. Equally damaging is degradation or ridicule, insults, and demonstrated or spoken hostility. Ignoring or leaving the elder out of normal conversations is another example of psychological abuse.

Material abuse. This form of abuse includes the illegal, improper, or unauthorized use of the resources of an adult for monetary or personal gain. It deprives the aged person of the use of resources accumulated for basic needs in retirement. Material abuse can involve the theft or misuse of money or property. It can be accomplished by force or through misrepresentation. Other examples would include fraud, misuse of Social Security funds, or forcing the elderly person to sign over legal title to property.

Medical abuse. This involves withholding medications or aids required, such as false teeth, glasses, or hearing aids.[4]

Though not usually listed as a formal category, other types of abuse could occur under a general heading of *violation of rights.* This would be the breaching of rights that are guaranteed to all citizens by the Constitution, federal statutes, federal courts, and the states. Examples would include having one's mail opened and censored, being refused access to a telephone, or not being allowed to receive visitors.

Self-neglect would include self-inflicted physical harm and the failure to take care of one's personal needs. It usually stems from the elderly person's diminished physical or mental abilities and can be intensified by the attitudes and behavior of the caretakers.

DESCRIPTION OF THE VICTIM

Most often the abused victim is a woman of seventy-five or more years, with one or more physical or mental impairments. Women are more likely to be abused than men because they live longer than men. Also, men who lose their wives tend to remarry younger women who take care of them. As a result, these men are not dependent on their children for help.

The female victim is found at all socioeconomic levels and in both urban and rural settings. She is most often widowed or single, and is heavily dependent on the family for her physical and emotional needs.

Most nursing care of the elderly occurs in a home. Of those persons living outside an institution, 5 percent are homebound. Also, about 85 percent have one or more chronic diseases that require continuing care. More than half of the care given the disabled in the community is provided informally by a spouse, relatives, or friends.[5]

A majority of the elderly are routinely being attended to by nonprofessional caretakers. This increases the chances for improper care, especially when the situation becomes chronic.

CHARACTERISTICS OF THE ABUSER

About 84 percent of the physical abuse of the elderly is committed by relatives. About 75 percent of those who are abused live in the same home as their abusers.[6]

The abuser and his family are usually experiencing a great deal of stress. Alcoholism, drug addiction, marital problems, and long-term financial difficulties all seem to play a role in bringing an individual to abuse his or her parent. Like child- and spouse-abusers, most people who are violent toward the elderly have histories of difficulty dealing with stress. They lack the ability to channel their anger in appropriate ways, and they aren't very effective at problem-solving.

The most likely abuser is the son of the victim. His form of abuse is usually physical. Daughters are the second most likely abuser, but tend to resort to psychological assault or neglect.

Abusers can also include spouses, grandchildren, siblings, roommates, and landlords.

WHY DO THEY ABUSE?[7]

As in all forms of family violence, there is no single explanation for why the elderly are abused. Any one or a combination of factors may explain violence of this kind.

Learned violence. Children may learn from their parents or extended family that violence is an acceptable response to stress and conflict. Reinforced by violent approaches to problem-solving seen on TV and within society, children grow up with a tendency to be violent.

The effects of child abuse earlier in life are very important here. One child in 400 who came from nonabusive homes will later attack his parents. In contrast, one out of two children who are mistreated by their parents will later resort to violence toward his parents.[8]

It could be described as retaliation, revenge, pent-up anger, or a learned response to frustration. The final product is an adult child who has a strong tendency to abuse his own father or mother. The pattern continues from one generation to the next (Exodus 20:5).

Dependent elder. Progressive and severe dependency also makes the elderly person vulnerable to abuse. Human nature tends to tolerate unkind treatment directed toward a more unfortunate person. An adult who pushes around an invalid is demonstrating the same quality that causes some people to beat up a drunken bum in an alley.

Violence can also result in the *learned helplessness* condition described earlier in regard to spouse abuse. As they become increasingly dependent, the elderly tend to believe they have no control over their lives, that they can do nothing to change their situations. They may even believe they have brought the abuse upon themselves. This keeps them from reaching out for help, since they tell themselves nothing will change anyway.

Many elderly victims see the family home as the only alternative to a nursing home or other dreaded institution. They are afraid of being taken away from loved ones, even if those relatives are abusive. So they quietly endure the abuse, believing no other options are available. They have learned to be helpless.

Lack of reconciliation. Another explanation is the failure of adult children to have resolved issues or feelings left over from previous conflicts, many of which probably took place during the teenage years. Adult children need to go beyond the stage of adolescent rebellion, to at last work through the emancipation struggle with their parents.

Usually the child leaves home, starts his own family, and visits on Thanksgiving and Christmas. And the relationship is relatively calm. But when the adult child becomes a caretaker for his parent, the old unresolved feelings emerge, making the use of

179

violence more probable. The same hostility can surface if there have been other unsettled conflicts, such as financial problems or parental disapproval of a child's choice of a mate.

Internal stress. Caring for a dependent, elderly relative can lead to accumulative stress for the family. In our mobile society, children tend to marry and move away from their parents. Instead of living close to parents and adjusting gradually to their aging, children are insulated from the process. When one parent dies or becomes disabled, leaving the other alone and dependent, a sudden and added responsibility is dumped on the adult children. These children, with their own lives interrupted, can become confused and resentful.

Out of obligation, the first step toward potential abuse is taken. The children make a hasty decision to have the aging parent come and live with them, though they later regret it. The increasing disability of the parent may interfere with the status quo of the family. Financial and emotional resources may become drained. Children may have to share rooms, or the parents may lose privacy. This triggers a combination of guilt and resentment which can be expressed in abuse of the aged parent.

These adult children, sometimes called the "sandwich generation" because of their position between their elderly parents and their children, are exposed to a unique set of stressors. They are confronted with the loss of youth, the recognition of their own aging, and the impact of an empty nest. All this takes place on top of caring for two sets of dependents.

These middle-aged children want the freedom to live as adults without the burden of aged parents in the home. In an attempt to deal with the conflict, the caretakers may overdose the parent with drugs, tie her to the bed, lock her in a closet, or threaten violence.

With increased pressure for two incomes, fewer daughters or daughters-in-law are free to be at home to care for the parent, creating added stress. After the stroke of a parent, for example, the adult children know they can't leave their mother alone. But they feel guilt, rage, frustration, and enormous fatigue after caring for her all night long and then having to go to work the next morning. Over an extended period, this can make some people resort to violence.

For example, a young woman beat her eighty-one-year-old

father with a hammer and then chained him to a toilet for seven days. She told authorities, "I worked him over real good. Then left him and rested. I watched TV for a while."

She was angry and worn out, but did not have the emotional or physical resources to do anything else but use physical abuse to get relief.

External stress. Another explanation for elderly abuse is external stress. Studies have shown elder abusers are likely to have alcohol- or substance-abuse problems. They may also be experiencing some form of external stress, such as the loss of a job or a long-term medical problem. Other examples of external stress are: troubles with a boss or coworkers, arrest or conviction for a crime, death of a close friend or family member, financial problems, pregnancy, in-law problems, separation, or divorce.

Any of these events, combined with a dependent parent, could bring about an overload of frustration.

Negative attitudes toward the elderly. Elder abuse may be reinforced by negative biases toward elderly people and their place in society. Our society idolizes youth and fears the advance of age and its attendant dependency. Such a negative viewpoint seems to have a correlation with the incidence of elder abuse in this country. In other parts of the world, where age and maturity are honored and revered, elder abuse is not the problem on the scale it has reached in America.

Perhaps we are paying the price for not following the Old Testament injunction: "Rise in the presence of the aged, show respect for the elderly and revere your God" (Leviticus 19:32).

REPORTING ABUSE OF THE ELDERLY

The victimized senior citizen rarely reports her abuse. The reasons are many: shame at being abused, fear of retaliation, and her belief that she is the major cause of the abuse and therefore deserves it. Sometimes victims of abuse do not have the physical ability to make a report, and some have been literally held prisoner and couldn't make a complaint if they wanted to.

All fifty states have mandatory reporting for child abuse. In 1980, only sixteen states had mandatory reporting laws for elder abuse. Between 1980 and 1985 that figure more than doubled, so that now thirty-seven states and the District of Columbia have some form of adult protective service laws.

There is little consistency, however, among these states as to who is required to report and what penalties will apply when there is failure to do so. For example, in Connecticut, everyone is required to report, but in New Hampshire, only physicians are included.

Since no consistently developed services exist to handle the reports, the plight of the abused adult is still a pathetic one. Cases abound where victims have come forward for assistance only to learn that nothing is available to help them out of their dilemma.

A major question is how to locate and identify the abused so intervention can take place in a timely and effective way. If the victim does not request help, it is hard to know what to do, especially since there is a constitutional guarantee against the invasion of privacy. Child abuse laws are enforceable without regard to the opinion of the victims. But unlike children, elders have the right to not press charges against their abusers. For example, the Massachusetts Community Reporting Law indicates that an elderly person has the right to refuse intervention even when subjected to abusive circumstances. This right must be protected. We don't want to remove one of the basic elements of free citizenship. However, we don't want to abandon our elders to the terror of abuse either.

The only recourse is to educate both the potential victims and those who care for them. Abuse of the elderly is a situation where intervention is negotiated, not imposed. The elderly person must be given acceptable options appropriate to his situation. A visiting nurse may strongly believe the elderly patient needs to be moved to a quality nursing home where his needs would be properly met. If the older adult doesn't believe that is an appropriate thing to do, he has the right to say so. The best that can be done is to make sure the person has had an opportunity to exercise choice, without coercion, and with a clear understanding of his alternatives.

Health-care providers such as nurses and doctors are the frontline observers for the detection of abuse. Much is being done by these professionals to increase their skill in observing and validating suspected abuse.

Pastors have a unique opportunity also. The pastor often has access to the elder adult through visitations. If he knows what to look for, any suspicions could be passed on to the proper authorities.

Because no well-defined system exists for reporting and investigating elder abuse in every state, the interested reader will need to take the time to find out the proper procedure for his particular locality. There may be a state commission on aging; if not, contact the Department of Health and Welfare.

DETECTING ABUSE OF THE ELDERLY

This section will describe a few of the most general symptoms of abuse that may be observed by visiting with an elder adult and his caretaker. Obvious instances of abuse will be self-evident. If you enter a home and see an elder adult chained to the toilet, you don't need a checklist to inform you of the abuse. The intent here is to help you be sensitive to the two major forces that produce abuse.

Abuse of the elderly seems more probable when the needs of the aged parent are great, and the ability of the family to meet those needs is inadequate. This suggests the two main categories for observation: (1) the needs and demands of the elder adult, and (2) the resources of the caretaker.

Severe abusers often have a history of violence, crime, or drug abuse. If you observe a family situation where the caretaker has such a history, be aware of the potential for abuse and neglect.

It is a good idea, if concerned about a situation, to inquire with the child protective workers in your area. If there has been any report of abuse to children, then elder abuse should also be suspected.

A pastor will often have opportunities to talk with members of families who consult him for a variety of reasons. As you talk with the caretaker, try to get an idea of the amount of stress present in his or her life. Look for the caretaker who is burning out. If your impression suggests high levels of stress and minimal levels of coping ability, look further at the implications for abuse or neglect.

Following is a list of observations that can be used where an elder adult is being cared for by someone else. The list is divided into two categories: items related to the elder adult and items related to the caretaker.

Symptoms in the Elder Adult

- [ ] Poor and deteriorating health
- [ ] Overly dependent on caretaker
- [ ] Was extremely dependent on spouse who is now deceased
- [ ] Persists in advising, admonishing, and directing the caretaker on whom he is dependent
- [ ] Has an unexplained or repeated injury
- [ ] Shows evidence of dehydration and/or malnutrition without obvious cause
- [ ] Has been given inappropriate food, drink, and/or drugs
- [ ] Shows evidence of overall poor care
- [ ] Is notably passive and withdrawn
- [ ] Has muscle contractures due to being restricted
- [ ] Views self negatively due to aging process
- [ ] Has negative attitude toward aging
- [ ] Insists on maintaining old patterns of independent functioning that interfere with caretaker's needs or endanger elder adult
- [ ] Intrusive; allows caretaker no privacy
- [ ] Is socially isolated
- [ ] Has no one to provide relief when uptight with caretaker
- [ ] Uses gifts of money to control others, particularly caretaker
- [ ] Refuses to apply for financial aid
- [ ] Savings have been exhausted
- [ ] Complains of loss of funds or property

Symptoms in the Caretaker

- [ ] Was abused or battered as a child
- [ ] Has a poor self-image
- [ ] Has limited capacity to express his own needs
- [ ] Was psychologically unprepared to meet dependency needs of elder adult
- [ ] Denies elder adult's illness or injuries
- [ ] Shows evidence of loss of control or fear of losing control

☐ Presents contradictory history or explanations for problems of elder adult
☐ Projects cause of injury onto third person
☐ Has delayed unduly bringing the elder adult in for care
☐ Shows detachment about problems or injuries
☐ Overreacts or underreacts to the seriousness of the situation
☐ Complains continuously about irrelevant problems unrelated to injury of elder adult
☐ Refuses consent for further diagnostic studies
☐ Views elder adult negatively due to aging process
☐ Has negative attitude toward aging
☐ Has unrealistic expectations of self or elder adult
☐ Is socially isolated
☐ Has no one to provide relief when uptight with the elder adult
☐ Is financially unprepared to meet dependency needs of elder adult[9]

There are no set guidelines, but if a number of items are observed in both the elder adult and caretaker, the question of abuse should be raised and appropriate action taken. The chief concerns are elderly adults with accelerating needs, who live with violent families, are being cared for by pathologic persons, or whose caretakers are under a lot of stress. If you observe such conditions, intervention may be necessary.

In closing, meditate on these verses:

Anyone who attacks his father or his mother must be put to death (Exodus 21:15).

He who robs his father or mother and says, "It's not wrong"—he is partner to him who destroys (Proverbs 28:24).

Do not cast me away when I am old; do not forsake me when my strength is gone (Psalm 71:9).

Honor your father and your mother, so that you may live long in the land the Lord your God is giving you (Exodus 20:12).

What can you do to help fulfill these commands? May God bless your efforts.

NOTES

1. Lee Pearson, "Elder Abuse: A Social Quandary," in *CARING*, vol. 5, no. 1, January, 1986, pp. 22-26.
   Jeanne Floyd, "Collecting Data on Abuse of the Elderly," *Journal of Gerontological Nursing*, vol. 10, no. 12, December, 1984, p. 11.
2. Select Committee on Aging, "Elder Abuse: A National Disgrace—Introduction and Executive Summary," reprinted in *CARING*, vol. 5, no. 11, January, 1986, pp. 5-7.
3. Val J. Halamandaris, "Elder Abuse: The Hidden American Scandal," in *CARING*, vol. 5, no. 1, January, 1986, p. 18.
4. M.R. Block, and J.D. Sinnott, eds., *The Battered Elder Syndrome: An Exploratory Study* (College Park, Md.: University of Maryland Center on Aging), 1979.
5. Lee Pearson, "Elder Abuse: A Social Quandary," in *CARING*, vol. 5, no. 1, January, 1986, pp. 23-26.
6. Suzanne Steinmetz, "Elder Abuse: One Fifth of Our Population at Risk," in *CARING*, vol. 5, no. 1, January, 1986, pp. 69-70.
7. The following section adapted from Grant L. Martin, *Counseling for Family Violence and Abuse* (Waco, Texas: Word), 1987, pp. 246-249.
8. Suzanne Steinmetz, "Battered Parents," in *Society*, vol. 15, July/August, 1978, pp. 54-55.
9. Adapted from Doris Ferguson and Cornelia Beck, "H.A.L.F.—A Tool to Assess Elder Abuse Within the Family," in *Geriatric Nursing*, September/October, 1983, pp. 301-305.

RECOMMENDED RESOURCES

The following resources are drawn from the expanding number of materials being produced in the area of family violence. The listings include books for children as well as adults. Many, but not all of the resources, have a Christian emphasis. Evaluate each resource carefully to see that it meets your needs and expectations.

1. Adams, Caren, and Fay, Jennifer. *No More Secrets: Protecting Your Child from Sexual Assault.* San Luis Obispo, Calif.: Impact Publishers, 1981.
   An extension of the practical suggestions for parents first outlined in *He Told Me Not to Tell.*
2. Bassett, Cary. *My Very Own Special Body Book.* Redding, Calif.: Hawthorne Press, 1981.
   Information about sexual abuse, incest, family roles, and how to protect oneself. Illustrated. Designed to be read to children.

3. Berry, Joy. *Alerting Kids to the Danger of Sexual Abuse.* Waco, Texas: Word, 1984.
   Written for children, it discusses types and causes of sexual abuse and how to ensure their own safety. Part of a "Danger Zones" series of three books. The other two are *Kidnapping* and *Abuse and Neglect.*
4. Byerly, Carolyn M. *The Mother's Book: How to Survive the Incest of Your Child.* Dubuque, Iowa: Kendall/Hunt, 1985.
   A practical survival guide, with state directory of services.
5. Carl, Angela R. *Child Abuse! What You Can Do About It* and related activity book, *Good Hugs and Bad Hugs: How Can You Tell?* Cincinnati: Standard Publishing, 1985.
   Very good material about child sexual abuse from a Christian perspective.
6. Davis, Diane. *Something Is Wrong at My House.* Seattle: Parenting Press, 1985.
   Book about parents fighting over children, grades 1–6.
7. Edwards, Katherine. *A House Divided.* Grand Rapids: Zondervan, 1984.
   A former missionary tells her story of incest and the widespread effects of unreported abuse.
8. Fay, Jennifer. *He Told Me Not To Tell.*
   A parents' guide for talking to your child about sexual assault. King County Rape Relief, 305 S. 43rd, Renton, Wash. 98055.
9. Fay, Jennifer, and Flerchinger, Billie Jo. *Top Secret.*
   Sexual assault information for teenagers only. King County Rape Relief, 305 S. 43rd, Renton, Wash. 98055.
10. Fortune, Marie. *Sexual Abuse Prevention: A Study for Teenagers.* New York: United Church Press, 1984.
    A five-session course for teens. Open-ended on issue of premarital sex.
11. Gil, Eliana. *Outgrowing the Pain: A Book For and About Adults Abused as Children.* San Francisco: Launch Press, 1983.
    A good secular book for victims.
12. Green, Holly Wagner. *Turning Fear to Hope.* Nashville: Thomas Nelson, 1984.
    A Christian discussion on spouse abuse and how the wife can break the cycle of violence.

13. Grossman, Rochel, and Sutherland, Joan, eds. *Surviving Sexual Assault*. New York: Congdon & Weed, Inc., 1983. Practical guide to preventing and surviving sexual assault. Includes listing of state-by-state resources.
14. Hyde, Margaret. *Cry Softly: The Story of Child Abuse*. Philadelphia: The Westminster Press, 1984. Study guide for ages 12-14.
15. Hyde, Margaret. *Sexual Abuse: Let's Talk About It*. Philadelphia: The Westminster Press, 1984.
16. Katz, William. *Protecting Your Children from Sexual Assault*. Little Ones Books, P.O. Box 725, Young America, Minn., 55399. A home Bible study including a parents' teaching guide and child's activity workbook prepared by members of the Christian Society for the Prevention of Cruelty to Children.
17. Kraizer, Sherryll Kerns. *The Safe Child Book*. New York: Dell, 1985. A common-sense approach to protecting your children from abduction and sexual abuse.
18. Martin, Grant L. *Transformed By Thorns*. Wheaton, Ill.: Victor Books, 1985. Victorious Christian living doesn't come by eliminating all our problems, but by learning how to apply godly principles to concerns such as stress, depression, self-esteem, worry, and anger.
19. Martin, Grant L. *Counseling for Family Violence and Abuse*. Waco, Texas: Word, 1987. Sixth book in the "Resources for Christian Counseling" series. Written for pastors and Christian counselors on topics of child sexual abuse, spousal abuse, and abuse of the elderly.
20. Miller, Kathy C. *Out of Control: A Christian Parent's Victorious Struggle with Child Abuse*. Waco, Texas: Word, 1984.
21. Miller, Kathy C. *When Love Becomes Anger*. San Bernardino, Calif.: Here's Life Publishers, 1985. Help with anger for frustrated mothers.
22. Morris, Michelle. *If I Should Die Before I Wake*. Boston: Houghton Mifflin, 1982. Intensely realistic fictionalization of father/daughter incest told through eyes of the daughter.

23. Peters, David B. *A Betrayal of Innocence.* Waco, Texas: Word, 1986.
What everyone should know about child sexual abuse. Strong Christian perspective.
24. Quinn, P.E. *Cry Out.* Nashville, Tenn.: Abingdon Press, 1984.
Dramatic account of abuse and neglect written from child's point of view by the victim himself.
25. Ricks, Chip. *Carol's Story.* Wheaton, Ill.: Tyndale House, 1981.
Personal account of suffering, guilt, and eventual spiritual freedom.
26. Sanford, Doris E. *I Can't Talk About It—A Child's Book about Sexual Abuse.* Portland, Ore.: Multnomah Press, 1986.
The story of a young victim. Written for children.
27. Sanford, Linda T. *The Silent Children: A Book for Parents about the Prevention of Child Sexual Abuse.* Garden City, N.Y.: Anchor Press/Doubleday, 1980.
28. Select Committee on Aging. *Elder Abuse: A National Disgrace.* Washington, D.C.: U.S. Government Printing Office, 1985.
29. Smith, Nancy. *Winter Past.* Downers Grove, Ill.: InterVarsity Press, 1977.
Story of repressed incest and victim's struggle with her faith.
30. Stowell, Jo, and Dietzel, Mary. *My Very Own Book about Me.* Lutheran Social Services of Washington, N. 1226 Howard, Spokane, Wash. 99201.
Workbook for children (ages 4-10), which teaches prevention skills and can be used in therapy. Both parents' guide and extensive therapists' guide available.
31. Strom, Kay Marshall. *In the Name of Submission.* Portland, Ore.: Multnomah Press, 1986.
Good resource for the battered wife who wants to honor God and also stop the pain.
32. Wachter, Oralee. *No More Secrets for Me.* Boston: Little, Brown and Co., 1983.
Positive and discreet stories about preventing sexual abuse for children, ages 6-12.
33. Williams, Joy. *Red Light, Green Light People.* Rape and

Abuse Crisis Center, P.O. Box 1655, Fargo, N.D. 58107. Coloring book for children which describes child molestation and good and bad touches.

ORGANIZATIONS DEVOTED TO FAMILY VIOLENCE, CHILD ABUSE, AND NEGLECT

American Association for Protecting Children, 9725 E. Hampden Ave., Denver, Colo. 80231; (303) 695-0811.
Provides information on the nature and extent of child abuse through books, reports, pamphlets, and other publications. Provides national leadership through training, consultation, research, advocacy, and information dissemination.

Center for the Prevention of Sexual and Domestic Violence, 1914 N. 34th St., Suite 105, Seattle, Wash. 98103; (206) 634-1903.
An interreligious educational ministry addressing sexual and domestic violence. Several publications available, including *Working Together,* a quarterly journal.

Center for Women Policy Studies, 2000 P Street, N.W., Suite 508, Washington, D.C. 20036; (202) 872-1770.
A feminist policy research center. Wide range of publications available, including *Response,* a quarterly journal dealing with the victimization of women and children and other topics.

Childhelp, U.S.A., 6463 Independence Ave., Woodland Hills, Calif. 91367; 1-(800) 422-4453.
Toll-free number for local child protective services agencies.

C. Henry Kempe National Center for the Prevention and Treatment of Child Abuse and Neglect, 1205 Oneida St., Denver, Colo. 80220; (303) 321-3963.
Provides training, technical assistance, and development of treatment programs for abused children. Rental of audiovisual materials available.

The Family Research Council of America, 515 Second Street, N.E., Washington, D.C. 20002; (202) 546-5400.
Christian lobbying effort on behalf of the family. Newsletter available.

Please Don't Hurt Me

Formerly Abused Children Emerging in Society (FACES), 71 Haynes St., Manchester, Conn. 06040; (203) 646-1222.
Self-help support group for young adults.

National Center on Child Abuse and Neglect, Children's Bureau, U.S. Dept. of Health and Human Services, P.O. Box 1182, Washington, D.C. 22013; (202) 245-2856.
Conducts research projects and administers federal funds for child abuse prevention and treatment programs.

National Center on Child Abuse and Neglect Clearinghouse, P.O. Box 1182, Washington, D.C. 20013; (301) 251-5157.
Dissemination resource for all types of books, pamphlets, reports, and instructional aids.

National Committee for Prevention of Child Abuse, 332 S. Michigan Ave., Suite 1250, Chicago, Ill. 60604; (312) 663-3520.
Coordinating body for state chapters and other organizations devoted to the prevention of child abuse and neglect. Catalog of publications available on request.

Parents Anonymous (P.A.), 22330 Hawthorne Blvd., Suite 208, Torrance, Calif. 90505; 1-(800) 421-0353.
Self-help organization for parents under stress.

Parents United/Daughters and Sons United, Adults Molested as Children United, P.O. Box 952, San Jose, Calif. 95108; (409) 280-5055.
Self-help support groups and treatment program for sexual abuse. Can refer to programs in local areas.

Seattle Institute for Child Advocacy, Committee for Children, 172 20th Ave., Seattle, Wash. 98122; (206) 322-5050.
Prevention of child abuse through school-based curriculum development, professional training, community education, and original research. Extensive educational materials available.

Sexual Assault Center, Harborview Medical Center, 325 Ninth Ave., Seattle, Wash. 98104; (206) 223-3047.
Numerous bibliographies and summaries of material on incest, sexual assault of children and adults, sex offenders, and the criminal justice system.